Makers of the Philharmonia

Galliera Susskind Kletzki
Malko Dobrowen Matacic Kurtz
Ackermann Fistoulari Weldon
Irving

Discographies compiled
by John Hunt

CONTENTS

3   Acknowledgement

4   Introduction

9   Alceo Galliera discography

43 Walter Susskind discography

77 Paul Kletzki discography

97 Nicolai Malko discography

113 Issay Dobrowen discography

129 Lovro von Matacic discography

137 Efrem Kurtz discography

151 Otto Ackermann discography

167 Anatole Fistoulari discography

185 George Weldon discography

203 Robert Irving discography

209 Index of composers and works

225 Credits

Makers of the Philharmonia
Published by John Hunt.
Designed by Richard Chluparty & John Hunt
© 1996 John Hunt
reprinted 2009
ISBN 978-0-952582-76-2

Sole distributors:
Travis & Emery,
17 Cecil Court,
London, WC2N 4EZ.
United Kingdom.
(+44) 20 7 459 2129.
sales@travis-and-emery.com

ACKNOWLEDGEMENT

This publication has been made possible by contributions from the following sponsor subscribers:

Richard Ames, New Barnet
Stathis Arfanis, Athens
Yoshihiro Asada, Osaka
Jack Atkinson, Tasmania
J.M. Blyth, Darlington
A. Brandmair, Munich
J. Camps-Ros, Barcelona
Edward Chibas, Caracas
F. De Vilder, Bussum
Richard Dennis, Greenhithe
John Derry, Newcastle-upon-Tyne
Erik Dervos, London
Hans-Peter Ebner, Milan
Shuntaro Enatsu, Miyakonojo City
Henry Fogel, Chicago
Peter Fulop, Toronto
Philip Goodman, London
Jean-Pierre Goossens, Luxembourg
Johann Gratz, Vienna
Peter Hamann, Bochum
Michael Harris, London
Donald Hodgman, Riverside CT
Martin Holland, Sale
Bodo Igesz, New York
Richard Igler, Vienna
Eugene Kaskey, New York
Shiro Kawai, Tokyo
Detlef Kissmann, Solingen
Eric Kobe, Lucerne
John Larsen, Mariager
Ernst Lumpe, Soest
John Mallinson, Hurst Green
Carlo Marinelli, Rome
Finn Moeller Larsen, Virum
Philip Moores, Stafford
Bruce Morrison, Gillingham
W. Moyle, Ombersley
Alan Newcombe, Hamburg
Hugh Palmer, Chelmsford
Laurence Pateman, London
Tully Potter, Billericay
Yves Saillard, Mollie-Margot
Helger Steinhauff, Stemwede
Yoshihiro Suzuki, Tokyo
H.A. Van Dijk, Apeldoorn
Hiromitsu Wada, Chiba
Urs Weber, St Gallen
Nigel Wood, London
G. Wright, Romford
A. Greenburgh, New Barnet

MAKERS OF THE PHILHARMONIA

When 10 years ago I collaborated with Stephen J. Pettitt on a discography of the Philharmonia Orchestra, it was still early days for the compact disc. We scarcely realised what potential there might be for re-issues of material from the mono LP era, let alone the earlier shellac period. In the intervening period the Philharmonia's recorded output with its major conductors has reappeared in CD format, so that virtually the complete discographies of Karajan, Klemperer and Giulini have become available both to collectors of the younger generation as well as to those of us old enough to have heard these conductors in their Philharmonia concerts in London's Royal Festival Hall.

Such was the healthy state of music-making just after the Second World War that there were sufficient talented musicians, many newly demobilised from military service, to form not one but two new ensembles to work alongside the three existing major London orchestras. Whilst the Royal Philharmonic Orchestra enjoyed the cachet of having Sir Thomas Beecham at its head, the Philharmonia emerged as virtual "house orchestra" for a powerful recording company under whose aegis the HMV, Columbia and Parlophone labels thrived in the healthiest of competition. A steady stream of recording assignments was available to the Philharmonia, not just with its principal conductors but also with a veritable host of highly talented orchestral trainers whose competence earned them the respect of the top international soloists who queued up to record with them. In the catalogues that follow you will therefore find the names of Heifetz, Menuhin, Oistrakh, Schnabel, Arrau, Gieseking, Callas, Schwarzkopf, Flagstad, Gedda, Christoff and Hotter, to list just a few. The discernment of Columbia's Walter Legge (also, of course, founder of the Philharmonia Orchestra) and his HMV colleagues in engaging the best conductors from home and abroad gives this EMI-based catalogue a guaranteed place in the annals of recorded sound.

I have compiled these discographies with the pleading of a particular cause in mind. Because many of the recorded jewels stem from the last days of the 78rpm era, and many more from the earlier mono period of the LP, there seems to be a wall of resistance among some collectors and re-issue companies against having anything but the most prestigious titles re-issued (Beethoven concerto recordings with Artur Schnabel, conducted by Dobrowen and Galliera, are such notable exceptions). It is being left to enterprising small companies, most particularly Testament, to investigate the material: they have issued three especially praiseworthy CDs devoted, one apiece, to the conductors Malko, Kletzki and Matacic.

Even more astounding than the neglect which I have just mentioned is what appears to be a head-in-sand outlook of the Philharmonia Orchestra's present management. They have issued several CDs of their own, to mark the orchestra's 50th anniversary, which are devoted to precisely the same material (with star names) that has already had maximum exposure from EMI! Philharmonia's archivist (I realise that they cannot probably afford to employ one!) has completely ignored the importance of the pioneering figures documented in this volume. Admittedly some of these men conducted the orchestra much more in the recording studio than in public, but they are still the ones who helped to build and concentrate the talents of Great Britain's most remarkable ensemble of instrumentalists.

The honour of guiding Philharmonia's very first steps in a recording studio - in July 1945 - fell to the Czech-born **Walter Susskind.** His output with the orchestra over the next 15 or so years was rivalled in quantity only by the Italian **Alceo Galliera** and the Pole **Paul Kletzki.** All three did of course also record with other orchestras both in London and abroad, but that work is not the subject of this volume. There is no doubt that their major achievements were with the Philharmonia. In Susskind's case this might be the Sibelius Violin Concerto with Ginette Neveu (now on EMI CDH 761 0112). Notwithstanding the continued availablity of the Callas recording of Il barbiere di Siviglia, which Galliera conducts, perhaps the best of this conductor still awaits re-issue, and I would cite a Respighi coupling (Pini di Roma and Impressioni brasiliane) in which the Columbia engineers achieve an exquisite balance of texture and atmosphere. Alternatively, there was a sparking collection of Rossini Overtures, which stand up well to later Philharmonia Rossini LPs with Karajan and Giulini. Galliera's Respighi

and Rossini records both re-appeared on EMI's
Music for Pleasure (MFP) label in the 1960s,
and are still to be found in second-hand record
shops - well worth the bargain price! Strangely,
Galliera did re-make certain Rossini Overtures
for stereo in 1959, but these were not published
until, some years ago, they surfaced on a
budget label CD compilation featuring various
conductors. In the case of Kletzki, Testament
has made it easier for today's listener by issuing
on CD two of his finest Columbia LPs, Tchaikovsky's
Manfred and Sibelius Symphonies 1 and 3.

Nearly all the conductors which concern us were
"plum label" artists, in no way a derogatory
term but reflecting rather a dependability and
adaptability which certainly did not preclude
inspiration. Furthermore, the contracts of
certain of the conductors allowed them to
"commute" between HMV, Columbia and even
Parlophone. This seemed to be an essential
requirement for ballet conductors in particular,
like **Anatole Fistoulari** and **Efrem Kurtz,** whose
fine Philharmonia LPs cry out for re-issue.
Similarly in need of investigation are the 78s
and LPs conducted by the Russians **Nicolai Malko**
and **Issay Dobrowen:** Testament has made a start
in the case of Malko, and Dobrowen deserves to
be remembered by more than the complete
Mussorgsky Boris Godunov which he conducted for
Boris Christoff with the Orchestre National in
Paris (Christoff and Dobrowen had, in fact,
already recorded the major scenes from the opera
with the Philharmonia, now on EMI CDH 764 2522).
Malko's Prokofiev collection (Symphonies 1 and 7
together with Love of 3 Oranges, now CDCFP 4523)
holds the distinction of being one of EMI's very
first published stereo recordings.

Up to around 1960 the EMI group seemed to hold
the monopoly on top-quality recordings of
Rimsky-Korsakov's Scheherazade. Apart from
Beecham's classic RPO version, there were
performances from the Philharmonia Orchestra
under no fewer than four maestri: Stokowski
(a version which soon reverted to the Victor
stable), Dobrowen (in my view the finest),
Kletzki and **Lovro von Matacic.** This did not see
publication of its stereo version until the
1970s but can now be heard in its CD incarnation
as beautifully passionate yet controlled in the
best Philharmonia manner (CZS 568 0982 or CZS
568 7392). Given the pedigree of some of these
conductors, Russian music in general seems to
have been a Philharmonia speciality at least as
far as the recording studios were concerned.
I can think of fine LP couplings which so far

have not re-appeared, like Dobrowen's Coq d'or and Tsar Sultan (surely the mono tag should not deter connoisseurs of such really cultured orchestral playing?) or Kurtz's Life for the Tsar (paired with the Ballet music from Gounod's Faust).

Lovro von Matacic was appreciated by Walter Legge for his experience in both opera and operetta, as was **Otto Ackermann,** chosen to direct a whole series of champagne operettas which helped launch the Angel label in the United States. Ackermann was also a model concerto accompanist, as can be heard in his poised backing for Solomon in the Mozart B-flat Concerto K450 (now on CDH 763 7072).

Last but not least, two of the many British conductors who produced fine results with the Philharmonia in EMI's studios: **George Weldon,** a specialist in lighter music of the highest quality (and with a long catalogue of records with Birmingham and Manchester orchestras as well) and **Robert Irving,** acknowledged to be the country's finest ballet conductor, although the United States probably appreciated his abilities more fully than we did ourselves.

As I write, I hear that one of Columbia's leading artists of the 1950s and 1960s has persuaded EMI to issue again a classic opera recording, long available in an early stereo remastering, in the version which most faithfully reflects the concern of producer and participants to obtain that meticulous blend and natural balance which were the hallmarks of EMI at that time. The recording in question now bears the legend "from the original mono tapes"! Perhaps a sign that the company will go on to re-assess their many fine Philharmonia recordings which have not seen the light of day since their original 78rpm or LP publication.

The discographies are arranged chronologically under composers and set out in three columns: first column gives the month and year of recording (venues were mainly London's Kingsway Hall and Abbey Road studios, with occasional excursions to Watford Town Hall), the second column indicates vocal or instrumental soloists and the third column the principal issue numbers for original and subsequent editions in various formats (78,45,LP,CD). I have tried to include as many US catalogue numbers as was possible, but am always glad to hear from American collectors who can add to my information.

John Hunt

Alceo Galliera
born 1910

PHILHARMONIA
ORCHESTRA

Anda

Concerto No. 2 in C minor — *Rachmaninov*
(Solo Piano: Preludes in G and G minor — *Rachmaninov*)
with the **PHILHARMONIA ORCHESTRA**
conducted by **Alceo Galliera**   33CX1143

Hungarian Fantasia — *Liszt*
Concerto No. 1 in E flat — *Liszt*
with the **PHILHARMONIA ORCHESTRA**
conducted by **Otto Ackermann**   33CX1366

Sawallisch

conducting the **PHILHARMONIA ORCHESTRA**
Symphony No. 4 in G — *Dvořák*
Scherzo Capriccioso — *Dvořák*   33SX1034

"Die Kluge" — *Carl Orff*
with a cast including Elisabeth Schwarzkopf,
Marcel Cordes, Gottlob Frick and Rudolf Christ   33CX1446-7

COLUMBIA
(Regd. Trade Mark of Columbia Graphophone Co. Ltd.)

33⅓ R.P.M. LONG PLAYING RECORDS

E.M.I. RECORDS LIMITED, 8-11 Great Castle Street, London, W.1

DANIEL AUBER (1782-1871)

La muette de Portici, Excerpt (Du pauvre seul ami fidèle)

April 1953	Gedda	LP: Columbia 33CX 1130
		LP: Columbia (France) 33FCX 302
		LP: Angel 35096/3204
		LP: EMI 1C 137 78233-78236/SLS 5250
		CD: EMI CDM 769 5502

JOHANN SEBASTIAN BACH (1685-1750)

Concerto in C BWV 1061

April 1956	Haskil, Anda	LP: Columbia 33CX 1403
		LP: Columbia (Germany) C 90519/33WCX 1403
		LP: Columbia (France) 33FCX 550
		LP: Columbia (Japan) XL 5183
		LP: Angel 35380
		LP: EMI SXLP 30175/1C 053 00439/ 2C 051 00439
		CD: EMI CDH 763 4922

LUDWIG VAN BEETHOVEN (1770-1827)

Symphony No 7

February 1950		78: Columbia DX 1697-1701/DX 8359-8363
		LP: Columbia (USA) RL 3035

Violin Concerto

July 1966	Grumiaux	LP: Philips SAL 3616
		CD: Philips 426 0642

12   Galliera

Piano Concerto No 1

February 1955	Anda	LP: Columbia 33CX 1302
		LP: Columbia (Germany) C 70431//33WC 533
		LP: Columbia (Italy) 33QCX 10194
		LP: Columbia (Japan) XL 5119
		LP: Angel 35248
May-October 1958	Arrau	LP: Columbia 33CX 1625
		LP: Columbia (Japan) OS 3054
		LP: Angel 35723
		LP: Columbia/Quintessence 7071-5
		CD: Pantheon D 15070
		CD: EMI CZS 767 3792

Piano Concerto No 2

May-October 1958	Arrau	LP: Columbia 33CX 1696/SAX 2346
		LP: Columbia (Japan) OS 3045
		LP: World Records T 568/ST 568
		LP: Columbia/Quintessence 7071-5
		CD: Pantheon D 15070
		CD: EMI CZS 767 3792
December 1970	Haebler	LP: Philips 6527 028

Piano Concerto No 3

April 1957-June 1958	Arrau	LP: Columbia 33CX 1616
		LP: Angel 35724/RL 3047
		LP: Toshiba AA 8015
		LP: Columbia/Quintessence 7071-5
		CD: Pantheon D 15070
		CD: EMI CZS 767 3792

Piano Concerto No 4

May 1955	Arrau	LP: Columbia 33CX 1333 LP: Columbia/Quintessence 7071-5 CD: Pantheon D 15070 CD: EMI CZS 767 3792
September 1955	Gieseking	LP: Columbia (Germany) SMC 91481 Cassette: EMI TCC2-POR 154 5949 CD: EMI CZS 762 6072
December 1970	Haebler	LP: Philips 6527 028

Piano Concerto No 5 "Emperor"

May 1947	Schnabel	78: HMV DB 6692-6696/DB 9326-9330 LP: HMV COLH 5 LP: Electrola E 90195/WCLP 577/ E 60623/WDLP 647/E 80485 LP: Toshiba GR 2001/GR 4006 CD: Testament SBT 1021
September 1955	Gieseking	Cassette: EMI TCC2-POR 154 5949 CD: EMI CDZ 762 6072/CDM 767 7962
June 1958	Arrau	LP: Columbia 33CX 1653/SAX 2297 LP: Columbia (Italy) 33QCX 10505/SAXQ 7372 LP: Columbia (Japan) OL 3177 LP: Angel 35722 LP: World Records T 645/ST 645 LP: Columbia/Quintessence 7071-5 LP: Toshiba EAC 30038 CD: Pantheon D 15070 CD: EMI CZS 767 3792

14   Galliera

Egmont Overture

June 1946   78: Columbia DX 1273
                                        78: Columbia (France) GFX 193
                                        78: Columbia (Italy) GQX 11100
                                        78: Columbia (USA) 72747D

Fidelio, Excerpt (Ach wär' ich schon mit dir vereint)

October 1950   Schwarzkopf   78: Columbia LX 1410
                                        78: Columbia (Austria) LVX 157
                                        45: Columbia SCD 2114
                                        LP: EMI EX 769 7411
                                        CD: EMI CHS 769 7412/CDM 565 5772

VINCENZO BELLINI (1801-1835)

La sonnambula, Excerpt (Ah non credea mirarti!)

October 1953   Dobbs   LP: Columbia 33CX 1305
                                        LP: Angel 35095

GEORGES BIZET (1838-1875)

Carmen, Suite

November 1956   LP: Columbia 33CX 1663/SAX 2303
                                        LP: EMI CFP 120

Carmen, Excerpt (Je dis que rien ne m'épouvante)

October 1950   Schwarzkopf   78: Columbia LX 1410
                                        78: Columbia (Austria) LVX 157
                                        45: Columbia SCD 2114
                                        LP: EMI ALP 143 5501

Les pêcheurs de perles, Excerpt (Je crois entendre encore)

April 1953	Gedda	78: Columbia LX 1614 45: Columbia SCB 118/SCD 2082 LP: Columbia 33CX 1130 LP: Columbia (France) 33FCX 302 LP: Angel 35096 LP: EMI 1C 137 78233-78236/EX 769 7411 CD: EMI CHS 769 7412

ALEXANDER BORODIN (1833-1887)

Symphony No 1

April 1955   LP: Columbia 33CX 1356
              LP: Angel 35346
              LP: EMI XLP 30107

JOHANNES BRAHMS (1833-1897)

Double Concerto

February-
March 1956
	D.Oistrakh,
	Fournier
		LP: Columbia 33CX 1487/SAX 2264
		LP: Columbia (Germany) C 90564/
		   33WCX 1487/C 70383/33WC 520/SBOW 8501
		LP: Columbia (France) 33FC 1048/SAXF 143
		LP: Columbia (Italy) 33QCX 10378/SAXQ 7264
		LP: Columbia (Japan) XL 140
		LP: Angel 35353
		LP: EMI 1C 037 01974/2C181 52289-52290/
		   XLP 30185/SXLP 30185/EMX 2035
		LP: Toshiba AA 8031
		CD: EMI CZS 569 3312/CDZ 762 8542

Tragic Overture

November 1956   LP: Columbia 33CX 1487/SAX 2264
                 LP: Columbia (Germany) C 90564/33WCX 1487
                 LP: Columbia (France) SAXF 143
                 LP: Columbia (Italy) 33QCX 10378/SAXQ 7264
                 LP: Angel 35353
                 LP: EMI XLP 30185/SXLP 30185

Galliera

ALFREDO CATALANI (1854-1893)

Loreley, Dance of the Water Sprites

November 1956
45: Columbia SEL 1618/ESL 6256
45: Columbia (Italy) SEBQ 204
LP: Columbia 33CX 1545
LP: Columbia (Italy) 33QCX 10330
LP: Angel 35483
LP: EMI 3C 053 01573

La Wally, Act 3 Prelude

November 1956
45: Columbia SEL 1618/ESL 6256
LP: Columbia 33CX 1545
LP: Columbia (Italy) 33QCX 10330
LP: Angel 35483
LP: EMI 3C 053 01573

La Wally, Act 4 Prelude

November 1956
45: Columbia (Italy) SEBQ 204
LP: Columbia 33CX 1545
LP: Columbia (Italy) 33QCX 10330
LP: Angel 35483
LP: EMI 3C 053 01573

FREDERIC CHOPIN (1810-1849)

Piano Concerto No 1

July 1956   Anda
LP: Columbia 33C 1057
LP: Columbia (Germany) C 70388
LP: Angel 35631
LP: Pathé TRI 33199
CD: Testament SBT 1066

FRANCESCO CILEA (1866-1950)

L'Arlesiana, Excerpt (E la solita storia)

April 1953   Gedda   LP: Columbia 33CX 1130
                                    LP: Columbia (France) 33FCX 302
                                    LP: Angel 35096/3204
                                    LP: EMI 1C 137 78233-78236/SLS 5250
                                    CD: EMI CDM 769 5502

CLAUDE DEBUSSY (1862-1918)

La mer

October 1950   78: Columbia DX 1726-1728/DX 8369-8371
                                    LP: Columbia (USA) RL 3055

Nuages (Nocturnes)

October 1950   78: Columbia DX 1754
                                    45: Columbia SED 5510
                                    45: Columbia (Italy) SEBQ 111
                                    LP: Columbia 33S 1002
                                    LP: Columbia (Germany) 33WS 1002
                                    LP: Columbia (Italy) 33QS 6003

Fêtes (Nocturnes)

October 1950   78: Columbia DX 1782
                                    45: Columbia SED 5510
                                    45: Columbia (Italy) SEGQ 111
                                    LP: Columbia 33S 1002
                                    LP: Columbia (Germany) 33WS 1002
                                    LP: Columbia (Italy) 33QS 6003

18 Galliera

Sirènes (Nocturnes)

October 1950   Glyndebourne   LP: Columbia 33S 1002
                 Chorus   LP: Columbia (Germany) 33WS 1002
                                     LP: Columbia (Italy) 33QS 6003

Prélude à l'après-midi d'un faune

February 1947   78: Columbia DX 1381
                                     LP: Columbia (USA) RL 3055

LEO DELIBES (1836-1891)

Lakmé, Excerpts (Sous le ciel étoilé; Les fleurs me paraissent plus belles; Pourquoi dans les grands bois)

October 1953   Dobbs   LP: Columbia 33CX 1305
                                     LP: Angel 35095

GAETONO DONIZETTI (1797-1848)

L'elisir d'amore, Excerpt (Una furtiva lagrima)

April 1953   Gedda   LP: Columbia 33CX 1130
                                     LP: Columbia (France) 33FCX 302
                                     LP: Angel 35096

La favorita, Excerpt (Spirto gentil)

April 1953   Gedda   LP: Columbia 33CX 1130
                                     LP: Columbia (France) 33FCX 302
                                     LP: Angel 35096

PAUL DUKAS (1865-1935)

L'apprenti sorcier

May 1959   LP: Columbia 33CX 1776/SAX 2419
                            LP: World Records T 582/ST 582

ANTONIN DVORAK (1841-1904)

Symphony No 9 "From the New World"

February-   78: Columbia DX 1399-1403/DX 8275-8279
March 1947

October 1953   LP: Columbia 33SX 1025
                            LP: Columbia (France) 33FCX 124
                            LP: Columbia (Italy) 33QCX 10128
                            LP: Angel 35085

MANUEL DE FALLA (1876-1946)

El sombrero de 3 picos, Suite

June 1946   78: Columbia DX 1258-1259
                            78: Columbia (France) LFX 761-762
                            78: Columbia (USA) MX 297

FRIEDRICH VON FLOTOW (1812-1883)

Martha, Excerpt (Ach so fromm)

April 1953   Gedda   78: Columbia LX 1617
                            LP: Columbia 33CX 1130
                            LP: Columbia (France) 33FCX 302
                            LP: Angel 35096

Galliera

CESAR FRANCK (1822-1890)

Symphony in D minor

March 1948   78: Columbia DX 1629-1633/DX 8340-8344
                                    78: Columbia (USA) M 15156-15160

Les Eolides

September 1947   78: Columbia DX 1507
                                    78: Columbia (Italy) GQX 11280

UMBERTO GIORDANO (1867-1948)

Andrea Chenier, Excerpt (Nemico della patria?)

October 1953   Panerai   LP: Columbia 33C 1052
                                    LP: Columbia (Japan) ZL 123

CHARLES GOUNOD (1818-1893)

Roméo et Juliette, Excerpt (Lève-toi, soleil!)

April 1953   Gedda   LP: Columbia 33CX 1130
                                    LP: Columbia (France) 33FCX 302
                                    LP: Angel 35096
                                    CD: EMI CDM 769 5502

EDVARD GRIEG (1843-1907)

Piano Concerto

September 1947	Lipatti	78: Columbia LX 1029-1032/LX 8579-8582
		78: Columbia (France) LFX 810-813
		78: Columbia (Italy) GQX 11163-11166
		LP: Columbia 33C 1040
		LP: Columbia (Germany) C 70095/
		    33WC 1040/C 91350
		LP: Columbia (France) 33FCX 322/
		    33FCX 491/33FCX 30096
		LP: Columbia (Italy) 33QCX 322/
		    33QCX 5026/33QCX 10213
		LP: Columbia (USA) ML 4525/3216 0141
		LP: Columbia (Japan) WL 5069/OL 3102
		LP: EMI XLP 30072/HLM 7046/1C047 00770M/
		    2C 061 00770/2C 051 43321/
		    1C 197 53780-53786M
		CD: EMI CZS 767 1632

April 1957	Arrau	LP: Columbia 33CX 1531 LP: Columbia (Germany) C 90904/33WCX 1531 LP: Columbia (France) 33FCX 745 LP: Columbia (Japan) XL 5234/ OL 3137/OL 2269 LP: Angel 35561

RUGGIERO LEONCAVALLO (1858-1919)

I Pagliacci, Excerpt (Si può?)

October 1953	Panerai	LP: Columbia 33C 1052 LP: Columbia (Japan) ZL 123

FRANZ LISZT (1811-1886)

Les Préludes

January- April 1953		LP: Columbia 33SX 1013 LP: Angel 35047 LP: EMI MFP 2087

Galliera

PIETRO MASCAGNI (1863-1945)

Guglielmo Ratcliffe, Intermezzo

January 1957
45: Columbia (Italy) SEDQ 204
LP: Columbia 33CX 1545
LP: Columbia (Italy) 33QCX 10330
LP: Angel 35483
LP: EMI 101 7691/3C 053 01573

Le maschere, Overture

January 1957
45: Columbia (Italy) SEDQ 689
LP: Columbia 33CX 1545
LP: Columbia (Italy) 33QCX 10330
LP: Angel 35483
LP: EMI 101 7691/3C 053 01573

JULES MASSENET (1842-1912)

Manon, Excerpt (Obéissons!/Profitons de la jeunesse!)

October 1953   Dobbs
LP: Columbia 33CX 1305
LP: Angel 35095

Manon, Excerpt (En fermant les yeux)

April 1953   Gedda
78: Columbia LX 1614
45: Columbia SEL 1590/SCB 118/SCD 2082
LP: Columbia 33CX 1130
LP: Columbia (France) 33FCX 302
LP: Angel 35096

Werther, Excerpt (Pourquoi me réveiller?)

April 1953   Gedda
LP: Columbia 33CX 1130
LP: Columbia (France) 33FCX 302
LP: Angel 35096

FELIX MENDELSSOHN-BARTHOLDY (1809-1847)

Violin Concerto

December 1946	Grumiaux	78: Columbia (Italy) GQX 11126-11129 78: Columbia (Switzerland) DZX 25-28

WOLFGANG AMADEUS MOZART (1756-1791)

Concerto for 2 pianos K365

April 1956	Haskil, Anda	LP: Columbia 33CX 1403 LP: Columbia (Germany) C 90519/33WCX 1403 LP: Columbia (France) 33FCX 550 LP: Columbia (Japan) XL 5183 LP: Angel 35380 LP: EMI SXLP 30175/1C 053 00439/ 2C 051 00439 CD: EMI CDH 763 4922

Alleluia (Exsultate jubilate)

May 1958	Moffo	LP: Columbia 33C 1061 LP: Angel 35716/60110/RL 3080

Ascanio in Alba, Excerpt (Perle di gioia)

February 1970	Hollweg	Philips unpublished

Così fan tutte, Excerpt (Una donna à 15 anni)

May 1958	Moffo	45: Columbia SEL 1690/ESL 6292 LP: Columbia 33C 1063/SBO 2754

Così fan tutte, Excerpt (In uomini, in soldati)

May 1958	Moffo	45: Columbia SEL 1667/ESL 6279 LP: Columbia 33C 1063/SBO 2754 LP: Angel 35716/60110/RL 3080

24 Galliera

Don Giovanni, Excerpt (Vedrai carino)

May 1958   Moffo   LP: Columbia 33C 1063/SBO 2754
                                     LP: Angel 35716/60110/RL 3080

Don Giovanni, Excerpt (Batti, batti)

May 1958   Moffo   45: Columbia SEL 1690/ESL 6292
                                     LP: Columbia 33C 1063/SBO 2754

Die Entführung aus dem Serail, Excerpts (O wie ängstlich!; Wenn der Freude Tränen fliessen)

February   Hollweg   LP: Philips 6500 042
1970

Die Entführung aus dem Serail, Excerpt (Welcher Kummer/Ach, ich liebte)

May 1958   Moffo   LP: Columbia 33C 1061

Et incarnatus est (Mass in C minor)

May 1958   Moffo   LP: Columbia 33C 1061
                                     LP: Angel 35716/60110/RL 3080

La finta semplice, Excerpt (Nelle guerre)

February   Hollweg   LP: Philips 6500 042
1970

Misera, dove son?, Concert aria

May 1958   Moffo   LP: Columbia 33C 1061
                                     LP: Angel 35716/60110/RL 3080

Nehmt meinen Dank, Concert aria

April 1955   Schwarzkopf   Columbia unpublished

Le nozze di Figaro, Excerpts (Deh vieni, non tardar; Non so più; Voi che sapete; Venite inginocchiatevi)

May 1958		Moffo			LP: Columbia 33C 1063/SBO 2754
					LP: Angel 35716/60110/RL 3080

Il rè pastore, Excerpt (L'amerò, saro costante)

May 1958		Moffo			LP: Columbia 33C 1061

Die Zauberflöte, Excerpt (Dies Bildnis ist bezaubernd schön)

February		Hollweg			LP: Philips 6500 042
1970

Die Zauberflöte, Excerpt (Ach, ich fühl's)

May 1958		Moffo			LP: Columbia 33C 1061
					LP: Angel 35716/60110/RL 3080

Zaide, Excerpt (Rase, Schicksal, wüte immer!)

February		Hollweg			LP: Philips 6500 042
1970

MODEST MUSSORGSKY (1830-1881)

Khovantschina, Entr'acte

September 1947			Columbia unpublished

Galliera

RICCARDO PICK-MANGIAGALLI (1882-1949)

Notturno romantico, Waltz

January 1957   45: Columbia SEL 1596/ESL 6256
                                45: Columbia (Italy) SEBQ 189
                                LP: Columbia 33CX 1545
                                LP: Columbia (Italy) 33QCX 10330
                                LP: Angel 35483
                                LP: EMI 3C 053 01573

ILDEBRANDO PIZZETTI (1880-1968)

La pisanella

April 1955   LP: Angel 35324

AMILCARE PONCHIELLI (1834-1886)

La Gioconda, Excerpt (Cielo e mar!)

April 1953   Gedda   LP: Columbia 33CX 1130
                                LP: Columbia (France) 33FCX 302/33FC 25098
                                LP: Angel 35096

SERGEI PROKOFIEV (1891-1953)

Violin Concerto No 2

May 1958   D.Oistrakh   LP: Columbia 33CX 1660/SAX 2304
                                LP: EMI SLS 5004
                                CD: EMI CZS 569 3312

GIACOMO PUCCINI (1858-1924)

La Bohème, Excerpt (Donde lieta uscì)

October 1950	Schwarzkopf	78: Columbia LB 110 78: Columbia (Germany) LW 51 78: Columbia (Norway) LN 5 78: Columbia (Italy) GQ 7246 45: Columbia SEL 1575/SCB 101/SCD 2141 45: Columbia (Germany) SCBW 101 45: Columbia (France) SCBF 108 45: Columbia (Italy) SCBQ 3001 LP: EMI RLS 763/154 6133

Madama Butterfly, Excerpt (Un bel dì)

October 1950	Schwarzkopf	78: Columbia LX 1370 78: Columbia (Italy) GQX 11456 45: Columbia SCB 102/SCD 2076 45: Columbia (Germany) SCBW 102 45: Columbia (Italy) SCBQ 3004 LP: EMI RLS 763/154 6133

Turandot, Excerpt (Signore ascolta)

October 1950	Schwarzkopf	78: Columbia LB 110 78: Columbia (Germany) LW 51 78: Columbia (Norway) LN 5 45: Columbia SEL 1575 45: Columbia (Germany) SCBW 101 45: Columbia (France) SCBF 108 45: Columbia (Italy) SCBQ 3001 LP: EMI RLS 763

28 Galliera

SERGEI RACHMANINOV (1873-1943)

Piano Concerto No 2

October 1953	Anda	LP: Columbia 33CX 1143 LP: Columbia (Germany) C 80109/ 33WSX 601/C 70438 LP: Columbia (France) 33FCX 281 LP: Columbia (Italy) 33QCX 10178 LP: Columbia (Japan) XL 5061 LP: Angel 35093 CD: Testament SBT 1064

Piano Concerto No 3

March 1948	Malcuzynski	Columbia unpublished

MAURICE RAVEL (1875-1937)

Daphnis et Chloé, 2nd Suite

January 1957	LP: Columbia 33CX 1663/SAX 2303 LP: EMI CFP 120

OTTORINO RESPIGHI (1879-1936)

Impressioni brasiliane

October 1950	Columbia unpublished
March 1955	LP: Columbia 33CX 1339 LP: Columbia (Italy) 33QCX 10206 LP: Angel 35405 LP: EMI MFP 2055

Fontane di Roma

March 1955	LP: Columbia 33CX 1339 LP: Columbia (Italy) 33QCX 10206 LP: Angel 35405 LP: EMI MFP 2055

NIKOLAI RIMSKY-KORSAKOV (1844-1908)

Capriccio espagnol

March 1955   45: Columbia SEL 1614
                                    LP: Columbia 33CX 1356
                                    LP: Columbia (France) 33FC 25092
                                    LP: Angel 35346

Le coq d'or, Excerpt (Hymn to the Sun)

October   Dobbs   LP: Columbia 33CX 1305
1953

Galliera

GIOACHINO ROSSINI (1792-1868)

Il barbiere di Siviglia

February 1957	Callas, Carturan, Alva, Carlin, Gobbi, Zaccaria, Ollendorff Chorus	LP: Columbia 33CX 1507-1509/ SAX 2266-2268 LP: Columbia (Germany) C 91030-91032/ 33WCX 1507-1509/STC 91030-91032 LP: Columbia (France) 33FCX 760-762/ SAXF 120-122 LP: Columbia (Italy) 33QCX 10297-10299 LP: Columbia (Japan) RS 3005 LP: Angel 3559 LP: EMI SLS 853/EX 29 10933 CD: EMI CDS 747 6348 Excerpts 45: Columbia SEL 1658/SEL 1662/SEL 1687 45: Columbia (France) ESBF 7110 45: Columbia (Italy) SCBQ 3065/ SEBQ 120/SEBQ 222/SEBQ 226 LP: Columbia 33CX 1790/SAX 2438 LP: Columbia (Germany) C 80634/ 33WSX 582/STC 80634/SHZE 101 LP: Columbia (France) 33FCX 30195 LP: Columbia (Italy) 33QCX 10443/SAXQ 7343 LP: Angel 35936/36293/3696/3699 LP: EMI SXLP 30166/SLS 5057/1C063 00735/ 2C 061 00552/1C 187 01398-01399 CD: EMI CDEMX 2123/CDCFP 4602/CDCFP 4613/ CDCFP 9013/CDC 555 2162/CDZ 101

Il barbiere di Siviglia, Overture

February 1950	78: Columbia DX 1690 45: Columbia SED 5517/SCD 2012 45: Columbia (Germany) SCDW 104 45: Columbia (France) ESBF 123 45: Columbia (Italy) SEBQ 120/SCDQ 2004 45: Columbia (Japan) EW 56 LP: Columbia 33SX 1006 LP: Columbia (France) 33FCX 208 LP: Columbia (Italy) 33QCX 208 LP: Columbia (Japan) XL 5054 LP: EMI MFP 2031

Il barbiere di Siviglia, Excerpt (Largo al factotum)

October 1953	Panerai	LP: Columbia 33C 1052 LP: Columbia (Italy) 33QC 5038 LP: Columbia (Japan) ZL 123

La boutique fantasque, arranged by Respighi

April 1953
- LP: Columbia 33S 1009
- LP: Columbia (France) 33FC 1031
- LP: Columbia (Italy) 33QC 5010
- LP: Angel 30001/35324

May 1959–
June 1960
- LP: Columbia 33CX 1776/SAX 2419
- LP: World Records T 582/ST 582

La Cenerentola, Overture

January 1953
- LP: Columbia 33SX 1006
- LP: EMI MFP 2031

La gazza ladra, Overture

February 1950
- 78: Columbia DX 1690
- 78: Columbia (Germany) DWX 5063
- 78: Columbia (Italy) GQX 11479
- 45: Columbia SCD 2085
- LP: Columbia 33SX 1006
- LP: Columbia (France) 33FCX 208
- LP: Columbia (Italy) 33QCX 208
- LP: EMI MFP 2031

May 1959
Columbia unpublished

Guilleaume Tell, Overture

January 1953
- LP: Columbia 33SX 1006
- LP: EMI MFP 2031

May 1959
- CD: EMI CDZ 767 2552

32   Galliera

L'italiana in Algeri, Overture

January 1953   78: Columbia DX 1910
                                    45: Columbia SED 5502
                                    LP: Columbia 33SX 1006
                                    LP: EMI MFP 2031

May 1959   CD: EMI CDZ 767 2552

La scala di seta, Overture

January 1953   45: Columbia SED 5502
                                    LP: Columbia 33SX 1006
                                    LP: EMI MFP 2031

May 1959   CD: EMI CDZ 767 2552

Semiramide, Overture

January 1953   LP: Columbia 33SX 1006
                                    LP: EMI MFP 2031

May 1959   Columbia unpublished

Il signor bruschino, Overture

January 1953   LP: Columbia 33SX 1006
                                    LP: EMI MFP 2031

CAMILLE SAINT-SAENS (1835-1921)

Havanaise for violin and orchestra

June 1956   Rabin   LP: Columbia 33CX 1597
                                        CD: EMI CMS 764 1232

FRANZ SCHUBERT (1797-1828)

Symphony No 5

April 1955   Columbia unpublished

ROBERT SCHUMANN (1810-1856)

Piano Concerto

May 1957   Arrau   LP: Columbia 33CX 1531
                                        LP: Columbia (Germany) C 90904/33WCX 1531
                                        LP: Columbia (France) 33FCX 745
                                        LP: Columbia (Japan) XL 5234/OL 3137
                                        LP: Angel 35561

IGOR STRAVINSKY (1882-1971)

L'oiseau de feu, Ballet suite (1919)

August–   78: Columbia DX 1757-1759/DX 8381-8383
December 1946   78: Columbia (Italy) GQX 11140-11142
                                        78: International Columbia DCZ 70-72

34 Galliera

RICHARD STRAUSS (1864-1949)

Don Juan

August 1946		78: Columbia DX 1356-1357 78: Columbia (France) GFX 166-167 78: Columbia (Italy) GQX 11146-11147
January 1957		LP: Columbia 33C 1060 LP: Angel 35784

Horn Concerto No 1

May 1947   Brain   78: Columbia DX 1397-1398
                             LP: Columbia (USA) ML 4775
                             LP: EMI RLS 7701
                             CD: Testament SBT 1009

Horn Concerto No 2

September   Brain   Columbia unpublished
1947   Recording incomplete

Oboe Concerto

September   Goossens   78: Columbia DX 1444-1446/DX 8301-8303
1947   78: Columbia (Italy) GQX 11193-11195
                             LP: Columbia (USA) ML 4775
                             LP: World Records SH 243
                             LP: EMI CLP 1698
                             CD: Testament SBT 1009

Tod und Verklärung

March 1955   LP: Columbia 33CX 1328
                             LP: Angel 35410

PIOTR TCHAIKOVSKY (1840-1893)

Piano Concerto No 1

October 1953	Anda	LP: Columbia 33CX 1156 LP: Columbia (Germany) C 70375/33WC 519 LP: Columbia (France) 33FCX 295 LP: Columbia (Italy) 33QCX 10095 LP: Columbia (Japan) XL 5060/ZL 111 LP: Angel 35083 CD: Testament SBT 1064
April 1960	Arrau	LP: Columbia 33CX 1731/SAX 2380 LP: Columbia (Germany) C 91133/STC 91133/ SAXW 9540/SHZE 161 LP: Columbia (Japan) OS 3029 LP: World Records T 581/ST 581 LP: Angel 60020 LP: EMI 1C 037 01697/1C 051 01697 LP: Toshiba EAC 30038

Violin Concerto

June 1956	Rabin	LP: Columbia 33CX 1422 LP: Angel 35388 LP: EMI MFP 2002 CD: EMI CDF 300 0212/CMS 764 1232

Capriccio italien

January 1953	45: Columbia SEL 1612 LP: Columbia 33SX 1013 LP: Columbia (France) 33FCX 239/33FC 25092 LP: Columbia (Italy) 33QCX 10074 LP: Angel 35047 LP: EMI MFP 2087

Romeo and Juliet

March 1955	LP: Columbia 33CX 1328 LP: Angel 35410

Evgeny Onegin, Excerpt (Faint echo of my youth)

April 1953	Gedda	LP: Columbia 33CX 1130 LP: Columbia (Germany) C 70411 LP: Columbia (France) 33FCX 302 LP: Angel 35096

36 Galliera

GIUSEPPE VERDI (1813-1901)

Aida, Prelude

January 1953

LP: Columbia 33SX 1009
LP: Columbia (France) 33FCX 209
LP: Columbia (Italy) 33QCX 10094
LP: Columbia (Japan) XL 5054
LP: Angel 35012

October 1958

Columbia unpublished

La forza del destino, Overture

June 1946

Columbia unpublished
Recording incomplete

January 1953

45: Columbia SED 5505
45: Columbia (France) ESBF 5119
45: Columbia (Italy) SEBQ 109
LP: Columbia 33SX 1009
LP: Columbia (France) 33FCX 209
LP: Columbia (Italy) 33QCX 10094
LP: Columbia (Japan) XL 5054
LP: Angel 35012

October 1958

Columbia unpublished

Luisa Miller, Overture

May 1959

Columbia unpublished

Nabucco, Overture

January 1953   78: Columbia DX 1904
                                45: Columbia SED 5505
                                45: Columbia (France) ESBF 5119
                                45: Columbia (Italy) SEBQ 109
                                LP: Columbia 33SX 1009
                                LP: Columbia (France) 33FCX 209
                                LP: Columbia (Italy) 33QCX 10094
                                LP: Columbia (Japan) XL 5054
                                LP: Angel 35012

May 1959   Columbia unpublished

Otello, Excerpt (Ave Maria)

October   Schwarzkopf   Columbia unpublished
1953

Otello, Excerpts (Credo in un dio crudel; Era la notte)

October   Panerai   LP: Columbia 33C 1052
1953   LP: Columbia (Italy) 33QC 5038

Rigoletto, Excerpt (Caro nome)

October   Dobbs   LP: Columbia 33CX 1305
1953   LP: Angel 35095

Rigoletto, Excerpt (Pari siamo/Figlia! Mio padre!/Chi è mai..lassù in cielo)

October   Dobbs, Panerai LP: Columbia 33CX 1305
1953   LP: Angel 35095

Rigoletto, Excerpt (Parmi veder)

April   Gedda   78: Columbia LX 1617
1953   LP: Columbia 33CX 1130
                                LP: Columbia (France) 33FCX 302/33FC 25098
                                LP: Angel 35096

Galliera

La Traviata, Preludes to Acts 1 and 3

January 1953		78: Columbia DX 1890
		45: Columbia SED 5517/SCD 2126
		LP: Columbia 33SX 1009
October 1958		Columbia unpublished

La Traviata, Excerpt (Addio del passato)

October 1950	Schwarzkopf	78: Columbia LX 1370
		78: Columbia (Italy) GQX 11456
		45: Columbia SCD 2076
		45: Columbia (France) SCBF 107
		45: Columbia (Germany) SCBW 102
		45: Columbia (Italy) SCBQ 3004
		LP: EMI RLS 763

La Traviata, Excerpt (Di provenza il mar)

October 1953	Panerai	LP: Columbia 33C 1052

La Traviata, Excerpt (Madamigella Valery?/Pura siccome un angelo/Dite alle giovane)

October 1953	Schwarzkopf, Panerai	LP: EMI EX 29 10753

Il Trovatore, Excerpt (Il balen del suo sorriso)

October 1953	Panerai	LP: Columbia 33C 1052
		LP: Columbia (Japan) ZL 123

I vespri siciliani, Overture

January 1953		LP: Columbia 33SX 1009
		LP: Columbia (France) 33FCX 209
		LP: Columbia (Italy) 33QCX 10094
		LP: Columbia (Japan) XL 5054
		LP: Angel 35012
May 1959		Columbia unpublished

RICHARD WAGNER (1813-1883)

Siegfried Idyll

January 1957   LP: Columbia 33C 1060
                                 LP: Angel 35784

Tannhäuser Overture

June 1946   Columbia unpublished

May 1947   Columbia unpublished

CARL MARIA VON WEBER (1786-1826)

Konzertstück for piano and orchestra

April 1960   Arrau   LP: Columbia 33CX 1731/SAX 2380
                                 LP: World Records T 581/ST 581
                                 LP: Angel 60020
                                 LP: Columbia (Japan) OS 3029
                                 LP: Toshiba AA 8015
                                 LP: EMI RLS 7712/1C 037 01697/
                                     1C 051 01697

Galliera

ERMANNO WOLF-FERRARI (1876-1948)

I gioielli della Madonna, Intermezzo

November 1956-
January 1957

45: Columbia SEL 1596/ESL 6256
45: Columbia (Italy) SEBQ 189
LP: Columbia 33CX 1545
LP: Columbia (Italy) 33QC 10330
LP: Angel 35483
LP: EMI 3C 053 01573

I quattro rusteghi, Intermezzo

June 1956

LP: Columbia 33CX 1545
LP: EMI 3C 053 01573

Il segreto di Susanna, Overture

October 1953

Columbia unpublished

June 1956-
January 1957

LP: Columbia 33CX 1545
LP: EMI 3C 053 01573

RICCARDO ZANDONAI (1883-1944)

Giulietta e Romeo, Cavalcata

January 1957

LP: Columbia 33CX 1545
LP: Columbia (Italy) 33QC 10330
LP: Angel 35483
LP: EMI 3C 053 01573

Columbia Stereophonic Discs*

*ON SALE DURING OCTOBER

 COLUMBIA

PICTURES AT AN EXHIBITION
—*Moussorgsky, orch. Ravel*
HERBERT VON KARAJAN
conducting the PHILHARMONIA ORCHESTRA SAX2261

SYMPHONY No. 1 IN C MINOR—*Brahms*
OTTO KLEMPERER
conducting the PHILHARMONIA ORCHESTRA SAX2262

'CELLO CONCERTO IN B MINOR—*Dvořák*
with Elégie—*Fauré*)
JANOS STARKER *with the* PHILHARMONIA ORCHESTRA
conducted by WALTER SUSSKIND SAX2263

'SONGS YOU LOVE'
ELISABETH SCHWARZKOPF *and* GERALD MOORE SAX2265

'THE BARBER OF SEVILLE'—*Rossini*
The cast includes MARIA MENEGHINI CALLAS,
TITO GOBBI, LUIGI ALVA
with the PHILHARMONIA ORCHESTRA
conducted by ALCEO GALLIERA SAX2266-8
(BOX SET ONLY: RECORDS CANNOT BE PURCHASED SEPARATELY)

PIANO CONCERTO No. 4 IN G—*Beethoven*
EMIL GILELS *with the* PHILHARMONIA ORCHESTRA
conducted by LEOPOLD LUDWIG SBO2752

'BEWITCHED' (Music of Richard Rodgers)
VICTOR SILVESTER *and his Silver Strings* SCX3254

'MILLION DOLLAR MELODIES'
RAY MARTIN *and his Orchestra* SCX3255

IMPORTANT:
These discs are for use with Stereophonic equipment only

PRICES, *including Purchase Tax:*
SAX 12-inch 41/8½ · SBO 10-inch 30/11½ · SCX 12-inch 35/10

33⅓ R.P.M. LONG PLAYING RECORDS
(*Regd. Trade Mark of Columbia Graphophone Co. Ltd.*)
E.M.I. RECORDS LTD., 8-11 GREAT CASTLE STREET, LONDON, W.1

Walter Susskind
1913-1980

PHILHARMONIA
ORCHESTRA

New Releases of Superb Stereo Discs by HMV

On sale during October

SIR THOMAS BEECHAM
Bart., C.H.

Royal Philharmonic Orchestra and Beecham Choral Society, Ilse Hollweg: (Soprano)

Music for
PEER GYNT—Grieg

ASD258

SIR MALCOLM SARGENT

B.B.C. Symphony Orchestra

SYMPHONY No. 1 IN E MINOR
—Sibelius

ASD260

CONSTANTIN SILVESTRI

Philharmonia Orchestra

SYMPHONY No. 5 IN E MINOR
—Tchaikovsky

ASD261

EFREM KURTZ

Philharmonia Orchestra

CLASSICAL SYMPHONY
—Prokofiev

SYMPHONY No. 1
—Shostakovitch

ASD263

YEHUDI MENUHIN

Berlin Philharmonic Orchestra conducted by Rudolf Kempe

VIOLIN CONCERTO
—Brahms

ASD264

ROBERT IRVING

Royal Philharmonic Orchestra

Ballet Music
MAM'ZELLE ANGOT
—Lecocq arr. Gordon Jacob

BIRTHDAY OFFERING
—Glazounov arr. Irving

CSD1252

MOURA LYMPANY

Philharmonia Orchestra conducted by Walter Susskind

CONCERTOS Nos. 1 & 3
—Prokofiev

CSD1253

TONY OSBORNE

His piano and orchestra

"OUR LOVE STORY"

CSD1254

KEEP IN TOUCH WITH YOUR RECORD DEALER

HIS MASTER'S VOICE Long Play 33⅓ r.p.m. RECORDS

E.M.I. RECORDS LTD., 8-11 GREAT CASTLE STREET, LONDON, W.1

TOMASO ALBINONI (1671-1751)

Oboe Concerto No 6

March   Goossens   78: Columbia DX 1753
1950

Oboe Concerto No 3, First movement

March   Goossens   78: Columbia DX 8368
1950   78: Columbia (Australia) DOX 1023

JOHANN CHRISTIAN BACH (1735-1782)

Sinfonia in B flat

July 1945   Columbia unpublished
                                    <u>Orchestra described for this recording as</u>
                                    <u>Philharmonia Chamber Ensemble</u>

JOHANN SEBASTIAN BACH (1685-1750)

Cantata No 51 "Jauchzet Gott in allen Landen"

May 1948   Schwarzkopf   Columbia unpublished

Cantata No 82 "Ich habe genug"

April 1948   Hotter   Columbia unpublished

46   Susskind

Erbarme dich (Saint Matthew Passion)

June 1950   Flagstad   78: HMV DB 21237
                                       45: HMV 7R 126
                                       45: HMV (France) 7RF 191
                                       LP: EMI HQM 1057/29 02061/
                                           1C 147 01491-01492M
                                       LP: Toshiba GR 2172
                                       CD: Testament SBT 1018

Double Violin Concerto

March 1946   Grumiaux,   78: Columbia DX 1276-1277
                 Pougnet   78: Columbia (France) GFX 124-125
                                       78: Columbia (Italy) GQX 11320-11321
                                       78: Columbia (Australia) DOX 854-855

Oboe Concerto, arranged by Tovey

June 1949   Goossens   LP: EMI CLP 1656/HQM 1087
                                       LP: World Records SH 243

Oboe Concerto in A

June 1952   Goossens   Columbia unpublished
                                       Recording incomplete

Piano Concerto in D minor

August 1946   Cohen   78: Columbia DX 1312-1314/DX 8242-8244
                                       78: Columbia (Italy) GQX 11223-11225
                                       78: Columbia (Australia) DOX 898-900
                                       LP: EMI HLM 7148

Suite No 2

August 1945   Columbia unpublished
                                       Orchestra described for this recording as
                                       Philharmonia String Orchestra

Violin Concerto in A minor

August 1951	Goldberg	78: Parlophone SW 8140-8141

Violin Concerto in E

May 1948	Goldberg	78: Parlophone SW 8108-8110 LP: Parlophone PMA 1007

LUDWIG VAN BEETHOVEN (1770-1827)

Piano Concerto No 3

June 1958	Firkusny	LP: Capitol P 8468/SP 8468 LP: EMI MFP 2040

Piano Concerto No 5 "Emperor"

April 1947	Matthews	78: Columbia DX 1462-1465/DX 8308-8312 LP: Columbia (USA) RL 3037

Violin Romance No 1

June 1950	Heifetz	HMV unpublished

Violin Romance No 2

June 1950	Heifetz	HMV unpublished

German Dances Nos. 11 and 12

April 1948		Columbia unpublished

Ah perfido!, Concert aria

March 1953	Hammond	LP: HMV BLP 1073

48   Susskind

VINCENZO BELLINI (1801-1835)

Norma, Excerpt (Sediziose voci!/Casta diva)

June 1949	Hammond Covent Garden Chorus	LP: EMI HLM 7042

HECTOR BERLIOZ (1803-1869)

La damnation de Faust, Excerpt (D'amour l'ardente flamme)

April 1953	Hammond <u>Sung in English</u>	LP: HMV BLP 1073

GEORGES BIZET (1838-1875)

Carmen, Excerpt (L'amour est un oiseau rebelle)

September 1951	Tourel	78: Columbia LX 1507 LP: EMI EX 769 7411 CD: EMI CHS 769 7412

Carmen, Excerpt (Je dis que rien ne m'épouvante)

September 1947	Steber	78: HMV DB 6514 78: Victor 12-0690 LP: EMI EX 769 7411 CD: EMI CHS 769 7412 CD: RCA/BMG GD 60521 CD: Metropolitan Opera CD 211

ARRIGO BOITO (1842-1918)

Mefistofele, Excerpt (L'altra notte)

March 1953	Hammond	78: HMV DB 21625

ALEXANDER BORODIN (1833-1887)

Prince Igor, Suite

June-September 1952		LP: Parlophone PMD 1023

MAX BRUCH (1838-1920)

Violin Concerto No 1

January 1953	Varga	LP: Columbia 33SX 1017
September 1956	Menuhin	LP: HMV ALP 1669/ASD 334 LP: Electrola E 70423/E 91055/ STE 91055/SME 91055 LP: EMI SLS 5106 CD: EMI CDM 769 0032/CZS 478 3092/ CZS 762 5362/CZS 767 3102 <u>Second movement</u> 45: Electrola E 41131 CD: EMI CDCFP 4332
July 1958	Ferras	LP: HMV ALP 1746/ASD 314 LP: Angel 35769 LP: EMI CFP 107

Ave Maria (Das Feuerkreuz)

March 1953	Hammond	LP: HMV ALP 1076 LP: EMI HQM 1186

ALFREDO CATALANI (1854-1893)

La Wally, Excerpt (Ebben? Ne andrò lontana)

June 1949	Hammond	78: HMV DB 21580 45: HMV 7R 172 LP: HMV ALP 1076 LP: EMI RLS 29 00143 CD: Testament SBT 1013

50 Susskind

GUSTAVE CHARPENTIER (1860-1950)

Louise, Excerpt (Depuis le jour)

| September 1947 | Steber | 78: HMV DB 6514
78: Victor 12-0690
CD: RCA/BMG GD 60521
CD: Metropolitan Opera CD 211 |

FRANCESCO CILEA (1866-1950)

Adriana Lecouvreur, Excerpt (Troppo, signori!)

| June 1949 | Hammond | 78: HMV C 3901
LP: EMI HQM 1186
LP: EMI RLS 29 00143
CD: Testament SBT 1013 |

Adriana Lecouvreur, Excerpt (Poveri fiori!)

| March 1953 | Hammond | LP: HMV ALP 1076
LP: EMI RLS 29 00143 |

ERNO DOHNANYI (1877-1960)

Konzertstück for cello and orchestra

| July 1956 | Starker | LP: Columbia 33CX 1595
LP: Angel 35627
LP: World Records T 783/ST 783
CD: EMI CZS 568 7452 |

GAETONO DONIZETTI (1797-1848)

L'elisir d'amore, Excerpt (Una furtiva lagrima)

| February 1946 | Nash
<u>Sung in English</u> | 78: HMV C 3492 |

ANTONIN DVORAK (1841-1904)

Cello Concerto

July 1956	Starker	LP: Columbia 33CX 1477/SAX 2263
		LP: Columbia (Germany) C 91018/ STC 91018/SAXW 2263
		LP: Columbia (France) 33FCX 725
		LP: Columbia (Japan) OS 3095
		LP: Angel 35417
		LP: World Records T 751/ST 751
		LP: EMI CFP 40070
		CD: EMI CZS 568 7452

Scherzo capriccioso

January 1946	Columbia unpublished
	Recording incomplete
July 1946	Columbia unpublished

The Cunning Peasant, Overture

January 1946	Columbia unpublished

Rusalka, Excerpt (God of the lake)

July 1958	Hammond	LP: HMV ALP 1680/ASD 302
	Sung in English	LP: World Records T 933/ST 933
		LP: EMI XLP 30205/SXLP 30205

Rusalka, Excerpt (Oft will he linger)

July 1958	Hammond	45: HMV 7ER 5118
	Sung in English	

Susskind

GABRIEL FAURE (1845-1924)

Elégie for cello and orchestra

July 1956   Starker   LP: Columbia 33CX 1477/SAX 2263
                                      LP: Columbia (Germany) C 91018/
                                          STC 91018/SAXW 2263
                                      LP: Columbia (France) 33FCX 725
                                      LP: Columbia (Japan) OS 3095
                                      LP: Angel 35417
                                      LP: World Records T 751/ST 751
                                      LP: EMI CFP 40070
                                      CD: EMI CZS 568 7452

CESAR FRANCK (1822-1890)

Variations symphoniques

June 1949   Lympany   78: HMV C 7784-7785
                                      45: Victor WHMV 1013
                                      LP: HMV CLP 1002
                                      LP: Victor LHMV 1013
                                      LP: EMI HLM 7179
                                      LP: Imprimatur IMP 5
                                      CD: EMI CDCFP 4650/CZS 568 1452

UMBERTO GIORDANO (1867-1948)

Andrea Chenier, Excerpt (La mamma morta)

July 1958   Hammond   LP: HMV ALP 1680/ASD 302
                                      LP: World Records T 933/ST 933
                                      LP: EMI XLP 30205/SXLP 30205

CHRISTOPH WILLIBALD GLUCK (1714-1787)

Orfeo ed Euridice, Excerpt (Che farò)

May 1948	Flagstad	78: HMV DB 6913
		45: HMV 7R 164
		LP: EMI HQM 1057/EX 29 02061/
		1C 147 01491-01492M
		CD: Testament SBT 1018

EUGENE GOOSSENS (1893-1962)

Oboe Concerto

April 1948	Goossens	78: Columbia DX 1578-1579
		78: International Columbia DCX 84-85

CHARLES GOUNOD (1818-1893)

Faust, Excerpts (Il était un roi de Thulé; O Dieu! Que de bijoux!)

| May 1949 | De los Angeles | 78: HMV DB 6938 |

Faust, Excerpt (Il se fait tard)

| February 1948 | Hammond, Nash, Brannigan
Sung in English | 78: HMV C 3724-3725
LP: EMI RLS 707 |

La reine de Saba, Excerpt (Inspirez-moi, race divine!)

| February 1946 | Nash
Sung in English | HMV unpublished |

Roméo et Juliette, Excerpt (Ah! Lève-toi, soleil!)

| February 1946 | Nash
Sung in English | 78: HMV C 3492 |

Susskind

ENRIQUE GRANADOS (1867-1916)

La maja y el ruisenor (Goyescas)

May 1949　　　De los Angeles　　　HMV unpublished

EDVARD GRIEG (1843-1907)

Peer Gynt, Suites Nos. 1 and 2

March 1956　　　　　　　　　LP: Columbia 33SX 1057
　　　　　　　　　　　　　　　LP: EMI XLP 30105/SXLP 30105
　　　　　　　　　　　　　　　Excerpts
　　　　　　　　　　　　　　　45: Columbia SED 5555/ESD 7256

Last Spring (Elegiac Melodies)

September 1947　　　　　　　Columbia unpublished

4 Norwegian Dances, arranged by Sitt

March 1956　　　　　　　　　LP: Columbia 33SX 1057
　　　　　　　　　　　　　　　LP: EMI CFP 40214

Symphonic Dance No 1

May 1956　　　　　　　　　　45: Columbia SED 5567/ESD 7259
　　　　　　　　　　　　　　　LP: EMI XLP 30105/SXLP 30105

Symphonic Dance No 2

May 1956　　　　　　　　　　45: Columbia SED 5567/ESD 7259
　　　　　　　　　　　　　　　LP: EMI XLP 30105/SXLP 30105

Symphonic Dance No 3

May 1956　　　　　　　　　　45: Columbia SED 5568/ESD 7260
　　　　　　　　　　　　　　　LP: EMI XLP 30105/SXLP 30105

Symphonic Dance No 4

May 1956   45: Columbia SED 5568/ESD 7260
                                             LP: EMI XLP 30105/SXLP 30105

Varen

May 1948   Flagstad   78: HMV DA 1904
                                             45: HMV 7EB 6011
                                             45: Victor WDM 1533
                                             LP: Victor LM 99
                                             CD: EMI CDH 763 3052

GEORGE FRIDERIC HANDEL (1685-1759)

Organ Concerto in B flat, arranged by Wood

June-   Thalben-Ball   78: HMV C 3814-3816
September
1948

FRANZ JOSEF HAYDN (1732-1809)

Violin Concerto in C

April   Goldberg   78: Parlophone R 20558-20560/
1947   SW 8098-8100
                                             LP: Parlophone PMA 1007

ERICH WOLFGANG KORNGOLD (1897-1957)

Die tote Stadt, Excerpt (Glück, das mir verblieb)

March   Hammond   78: HMV DB 21625
1953   LP: EMI EX 769 7411
                                             CD: EMI CHS 769 7412

Susskind

EDOUARD LALO (1823-1892)

Symphonie espagnole

June 1950	Heifetz	HMV unpublished
July 1958	Ferras	LP: HMV ALP 1746/ASD 314 LP: Angel 35769 LP: EMI CFP 107

RUGGIERO LEONCAVALLO (1858-1919)

I Pagliacci, Excerpt (O Colombina!/ E dessa!)

June 1948	Hammond, Hargreaves <u>Sung in English</u>	78: HMV C 3923-3924 <u>E dessa only</u> LP: EMI HQM 1089

FRANZ LISZT (1811-1886)

Piano Concerto No 2

September 1947	Malcuzynski	78: Columbia LX 1071-1073/LX 8605-8607 78: Columbia (France) LFX 770-772 78: Columbia (Italy) GQX 11214-11216 78: Columbia (USA) M 777/D 227
March 1953	Malcuzynski	LP: Columbia 33CX 1106 LP: Columbia (USA) ML 4146

Hungarian Fantasia for piano and orchestra

April 1948	Solomon	78: HMV C 3761-3762/C 7688-7689 45: HMV 7EP 7132 LP: World Records SH 125 LP: EMI RLS 701/SLS 5094 LP: Turnabout THS 65108 CD: EMI CDH 763 8212

Hungarian Rhapsody No 2

June 1947		Columbia unpublished <u>Recording incomplete</u>

HENRY LITOLFF (1818-1891)

Scherzo (Concerto symphonique No 4)

April 1948	Lympany	78: HMV C 3763 78: Victor 12-1496 45: HMV 7P 105/7P 225/7EP 7014 45: HMV (France) 7BF 1053 45: HMV (Italy) 7PQ 2012/7EPQ 528 LP: EMI HLM 7179 LP: Imprimatur IMP 5 CD: EMI CDCFP 4650/CZS 568 1452

ALESSANDRO MARCELLO (1684-1750)

Oboe Concerto in D minor

April 1947	Goossens	78: Columbia DX 1389-1390

PIETRO MASCAGNI (1863-1945)

Cavalleria rusticana, Excerpt (Easter Hymn)

January 1946	Hobson, Ripley Chorus Sung in English	Columbia unpublished
July 1958	Hammond Chorus	LP: HMV ALP 1680/ASD 302 LP: World Records T 933/ST 933 LP: EMI XLP 30205/SXLP 30205

Cavalleria rusticana, Excerpt (Voi lo sapete)

June 1948	Hammond Sung in English	78: HMV C 3771

JULES MASSENET (1842-1912)

Manon, Excerpt (En fermant les yeux)

May 1949	Schock	78: HMV B 9868
		78: Electrola DA 5511
		LP: EMI 1C 147 28963-28964/EX 29 12013
August 1951	Midgeley <u>Sung in English</u>	78: HMV DB 21358
		LP: EMI HQM 1228

Manon, Excerpt (Adieu, notre petite table)

May 1949	De los Angeles	78: HMV DB 6994
March 1953	Hammond	LP: HMV ALP 1076

Manon, Excerpt (Ah fuyez, doux image!)

August 1951	Midgeley <u>Sung in English</u>	78: HMV DB 21358

Manon, Excerpt (Je suis encore tout étourdie)

March 1953	Hammond	LP: HMV ALP 1076

Thais, Excerpt (L'amour est une vertu rare)

March 1953	Hammond	LP: HMV ALP 1076

FELIX MENDELSSOHN-BARTHOLDY (1809-1847)

Hebrides, Overture

September 1952	Columbia unpublished

DARIUS MILHAUD (1892-1974)

Cello Concerto

July 1956	Starker	LP: Columbia 33CX 1425 CD: EMI CZS 568 7452

WOLFGANG AMADEUS MOZART (1756-1791)

Horn Concerto No 2

March 1946	Brain	78: Columbia DX 1365-1366 78: Columbia (Italy) GQX 11480-11481 78: Columbia (USA) MX 306 LP: Columbia (USA) ML 2088 LP: EMI HQM 1033/RLS 7701 LP: Angel 60040 CD: EMI CDH 764 1982

Piano Concerto No 9

May 1948	L.Kraus	78: Parlophone SW 8104-8106

Piano Concerto No 20

June 1948	Schnabel	45: Victor WHMV 1012 LP: Victor LHMV 1012 LP: HMV (France) FJLP 5014 LP: EMI 2C 051 43166/EX 29 00723 LP: Turnabout THS 65046 CD: Arabesque Z 6591 CD: EMI CHS 763 7032

Piano Concerto No 24

June 1948	Schnabel	45: Victor WHMV 1012 LP: Victor LHMV 1012 LP: HMV (France) FJLP 5014 LP: EMI 2C 051 43166/EX 29 00723 LP: Turnabout THS 65046 CD: Arabesque Z 6592 CD: EMI CHS 763 7032

60   Susskind

Violin Concerto No 1

January   Varga   LP: Columbia 33SX 1017
1953

Violin Concerto No 3

August   Goldberg   LP: Parlophone PMA 1003
1951   LP: Toshiba EAC 60230-60239
                               CD: Testament SBT 1028

Violin Concerto No 4

August   Goldberg   LP: Parlophone PMA 1003
1951   LP: Toshiba EAC 60230-60239
                               CD: Testament SBT 1028

Violin Concerto No 5

August   Goldberg   CD: Testament SBT 1028
1951

Cosl fan tutte, Excerpts (In uomini, in soldati;   Una donna a 15 anni)

September   Noni   78: HMV DA 1986
1950   CD: Testament SBT 1040

Don Giovanni, Excerpt (Dalla sua pace)

August   Midgley   LP: EMI EX 769 7411
1951   CD: EMI CHS 769 7412
                               Orchestra and conductor incorrectly
                               described as Covent Garden/Goodall

Exsultate jubilate

May 1948	Schwarzkopf	78: Columbia LX 1196-1197
		LP: Columbia (USA) ML 4649
		LP: Columbia (Germany) C 80628
		LP: Angel 60013
		LP: EMI RLS 154 6133
		CD: EMI CDH 763 2012

Misera, dove son?, Concert aria

| March 1953 | Hammond | LP: HMV ALP 1076 |

Le nozze di Figaro, Overture

| September 1952 | | 78: Columbia DX 8405 |
| | | 78: Columbia (Australia) DOX 1016 |

Le nozze di Figaro, Excerpt (Porgi amor)

September 1947	Baillie Sung in English	Columbia unpublished
September 1947	Steber	HMV unpublished
May 1949	De los Angeles	78: HMV DB 6994
		LP: EMI SLS 5233/EX 29 05583

Le nozze di Figaro, Excerpt (Voi che sapete)

| May 1949 | De los Angeles | HMV unpublished |

Le nozze di Figaro, Excerpt (Dove sono)

| September 1947 | Baillie Sung in English | 78: Columbia DB 2444 |
| September 1947 | Steber | HMV unpublished |

MODEST MUSSORGSKY (1839-1881)

Boris Godunov, Introduction, Polonaise and March

March 1953	Parlophone unpublished

The Capture of Kars, Triumphal March arranged by Rimsky-Korsakov

March 1953	LP: Parlophone PMC 1018 LP: EMI MFP 2049

Intermezzo in B minor, arranged by Rimsky-Korsakov

March 1953	LP: Parlophone PMC 1018 LP: EMI MFP 2049

Khovantschina, Prelude, Dance of Persian Slaves and Entr'acte

March 1953	LP: Parlophone PMC 1018 LP: EMI MFP 2049

Night on Bare Mountain

March 1953	LP: Parlophone PMC 1018 LP: EMI MFP 2049

Scherzo in B flat, arranged by Rimsky-Korsakov

March 1953	LP: Parlophone PMC 1018 LP: EMI MFP 2049

Sorochintsky Fair, Introduction and Gopak, arranged by Liadov

March 1953	LP: Parlophone PMC 1018 LP: EMI MFP 2049

SERGEI PROKOFIEV (1891-1953)

Piano Concerto No 1

| May 1956 | Lympany | LP: HMV CLP 1126/CSD 1253
LP: World Records T 735/ST 735
CD: Olympia OCD 190 |

Piano Concerto No 3

| May 1956 | Lympany | LP: HMV CLP 1126/CSD 1253
LP: World Records T 735/ST 735
CD: Olympia OCD 191 |

Cello Concerto in E minor

| July 1956 | Starker | LP: Columbia 33CX 1425
LP: Angel 35418
LP: Columbia (Japan) OL 3201
CD: EMI CZS 568 7452 |

GIACOMO PUCCINI (1858-1924)

La Bohème, Excerpt (Quando me'n vo')

| September 1951 | Tourel | 78: Columbia LX 1507 |

La Bohème, Excerpt (Mi chiamano Mimì)

| May 1949 | De los Angeles | HMV unpublished |

La fanciulla del West, Excerpt (Laggiù nel soledad)

| February 1946 | Hammond
<u>Sung in English</u> | LP: EMI HLM 7042 |

Susskind

Madama Butterfly, Excerpt (Ancora un passo)

July 1958	Hammond Chorus	LP: HMV ALP 1680/ASD 302 LP: World Records T 933/ST 933 LP: EMI XLP 30205/SXLP 30205

Madama Butterfly, Excerpt (Che tua madre)

February 1946	Hammond Sung in English	HMV unpublished

Manon Lescaut, Excerpt (Sola perduta abandonata)

July 1958	Hammond	LP: HMV ALP 1680/ASD 302 LP: World Records T 933/ST 933 LP: EMI XLP 30205/SXLP 30205/RLS 29 00143

Tosca, Excerpt (Vissi d'arte)

May 1948	Welitsch	78: Columbia LB 82 78: Columbia (Australia) LO 90 LP: EMI HLM 7006/101 2671/ 1C 047 01267M LP: Angel 60202 LP: World Records SH 289 CD: EMI CDH 761 0072

Tosca, Excerpt (E lucevan le stelle)

May 1949	Schock	78: HMV B 9868 78: Electrola DA 5511 LP: EMI 1C 147 28963-28964/EX 29 12013

Tosca, Excerpt (Non la sospiri)

February 1948	Hammond, Nash Sung in English	78: HMV B 9705

Turandot, Excerpt (In questa reggia)

July 1958   Hammond   LP: HMV ALP 1680/ASD 302
                                      LP: World Records T 933/ST 933
                                      LP: EMI XLP 30205/SXLP 30205

Turandot, Excerpt (Non piangere Liù)

May 1949   Schock   78: Electrola DA 5512
                                      LP: EMI 1C 147 28963-28964/EX 29 12013

Turandot, Excerpt (Nessun dorma)

May 1949   Schock   78: Electrola DA 5512
                                      LP: EMI 1C 147 28963-28964/EX 29 12013
                                      CD: EMI CZS 767 1832

SERGEI RACHMANINOV (1873-1943)

Piano Concerto No 3

September   Pennario   LP: Capitol P 8524/SP 8524
1959   CD: EMI CDEMX 2138/CDM 762 0472

Rhapsody on a theme of Paganini

September   Rubinstein   78: HMV DB 6556-6558/DB 9188-9190
1947   78: Victor M 1269
                                      45: Victor WDM 1269
                                      LP: Victor LM 26
                                      LP: HMV (France) FALP 253/FBLP 1021
                                      LP: EMI EX 154 4273

66   Susskind

CAMILLE SAINT-SAENS (1835-1921)

Cello Concerto No 1

September 1947	Fournier	78: HMV DB 6602-6603

Etienne Marcel, Excerpt (O beaux rêves évanouis)

March 1953	Hammond	LP: HMV BLP 1073 CD: Testament SBT 1013

Samson et Dalila, Excerpts (Printemps qui commence; Mon coeur s'ouvre à ta voix)

September 1951	Tourel	78: Columbia LX 1555

DOMENICO SCARLATTI (1685-1757)

Oboe Concerto, arranged by Bryan

April 1947- May 1949	Goossens	78: Columbia DX 8347-8348

JEAN SIBELIUS (1865-1957)

Violin Concerto

November 1945	Neveu	78: HMV DB 6244-6247/DB 9007-9010 LP: HMV ALP 1479 LP: Electrola E 60586/WDLP 622 LP: HMV (France) FJLP 5036 LP: Columbia (Argentina) LPC 11575 LP: Toshiba GR 2084 LP: EMI RLS 739/EX 29 08241 CD: EMI CDH 761 0112 <u>Philharmonia Orchestra's first major recording project</u>

BEDRICH SMETANA (1824-1884)

The Bartered Bride, Excerpt (Alone at last/Our dream of love)

July 1958   Hammond   LP: HMV ALP 1680/ASD 302
              <u>Sung in English</u>   LP: World Records T 933/ST 933
                                  LP: EMI XLP 30205/SXLP 30205

Dalibor, Excerpt (Do I live?)

July 1958   Hammond   LP: HMV ALP 1680/ASD 302
              <u>Sung in English</u>   LP: World Records T 933/ST 933
                                  LP: EMI XLP 30205/SXLP 30205

JOHANN STRAUSS (1825-1899)

Frühlingsstimmen, Waltz

May 1949   Berger   78: HMV DB 6954
                              CD: EMI CDM 763 7592

GIUSEPPE TARTINI (1692-1770)

Concertino, arranged by Jacob

August   Columbia unpublished
1945   <u>Orchestra described for this recording as</u>
                                   <u>Philharmonia String Orchestra</u>

68   Susskind

PIOTR TCHAIKOVSKY (1840-1893)

Violin Concerto

June 1950	Heifetz	78: HMV DB 21228-21231
		78: Victor DM 1442
		45: Victor WDM 1442
		LP: HMV BLP 1012
		LP: Victor LM 1111
		LP: HMV (France) FBLP 1008
		LP: HMV (Italy) QBLP 1008
		LP: HMV (Austria) VBLP 801
		LP: RCA ARM4-0947
		LP: RCA (Spain) 3L-16222
		CD: RCA/BMG 09026 617782

Evgeny Onegin, Excerpt (Tatiana's Letter scene)

May 1948	Welitsch Sung in German	78: Columbia LX 1108-1109
		78: Columbia (USA) X 310
		LP: Columbia 33C 1011
		LP: Columbia (Austria) 33VC 806
		LP: Columbia (USA) ML 2048/ML 4795
		LP: World Records SH 289
		LP: Angel 60202
		LP: EMI HLM 7006/101 2671/ 1C 047 01267M
		CD: EMI CDH 761 0072/CHS 764 8552
July 1958	Hammond Sung in English	LP: HMV ALP 1680/ASD 302
		LP: World Records T 933/ST 933
		LP: EMI XLP 30205/SXLP 30205

The Maid of Orleans, Excerpt (Adieu forêts!)

September 1951	Tourel	Columbia unpublished

Pique Dame, Excerpt (T'will soon be midnight)

July 1958	Hammond Sung in English	LP: HMV ALP 1680/ASD 302
		LP: World Records T 933/ST 933
		LP: EMI XLP 30205/SXLP 30205

JOAQUIN TURINA (1882-1949)

Saeta en forma de salve a la virgen de la esperanza

May 1949	De los Angeles	78: HMV DA 1929 CD: EMI CDH 764 0282

Cantares (Poema en forma de canciones)

May 1949	De los Angeles	78: HMV DA 1929 CD: EMI CDH 764 0282

Rapsodia sinfonica for piano and orchestra

June 1949	Łympany	78: HMV C 3913/DB 4306 LP: Victor LHMV 1025 Cassette: Imprimatur DIMP 2

RALPH VAUGHAN WILLIAMS (1872-1958)

Oboe Concerto

June- September 1951	Goossens	LP: World Records SH 243

GIUSEPPE VERDI (1813-1901)

Aida, Excerpt (O patria mia)

| April 1953 | Hammond | 78: HMV DB 21580 |

Un ballo in maschera, Excerpt (Ecco l'orrido campo!)

| June 1948 | Hammond
Sung in English | 78: HMV C 3771 |

Un ballo in maschera, Excerpts (Volta la terra; Saper vorreste)

| September 1950 | Noni | 78: HMV DA 1954 |

La forza del destino, Excerpt (Son giunta!/Madre pietosa vergine)

| June 1949 | Hammond
Covent Garden
Chorus | 78: HMV DB 21019
45: HMV 7ER 5077
LP: EMI HQM 1186/RLS 29 00143 |

Ingemisco (Requiem)

| September 1948 | Nash | 78: HMV B 9705 |

Rigoletto, Excerpt (Caro nome)

| May 1949 | Berger | HMV unpublished |

Rigoletto, Excerpt (Pari siamo)

| September 1950 | Gobbi | 78: HMV DB 21227
LP: EMI RLS 738/1C 187 01549-01550
CD: Testament SBT 1019 |

Otello, Excerpt (Willow Song and Ave Maria)

May 1950	Hammond, Sinclair	HMV unpublished

La Traviata, Excerpt (E strano!/Follie!/Sempre libera)

February 1946	Hammond <u>Sung in English</u>	78: HMV C 3486 78: Columbia (Australia) EB 360

La Traviata, Excerpt (Di provenza il mar)

September 1950	Gobbi	78: HMV DB 21227 LP: EMI RLS 738/1C 187 01549-01550 CD: Testament SBT 1019

HENRI VIEUXTEMPS (1820-1881)

Violin Concerto No 4

May 1951	Menuhin	78: HMV DB 21307-21309 LP: HMV BLP 1005

ANTONIO VIVALDI (1678-1741)

Oboe Concerto in D minor

June 1949	Goossens	78: Columbia DX 8367-8368 78: Columbia (Italy) GQX 11457-11458

Susskind

RICHARD WAGNER (1813-1883)

Der fliegende Holländer, Excerpt (Traft ihr das Schiff)

January 1946	Hobson	Columbia unpublished

Lohengrin, Excerpt (Einsam in trüben Tagen)

April 1956	Schwarzkopf	LP: Columbia 33CX 1658/SAX 2300 LP: Columbia (France) 33FCX 821 LP: Angel 35806 LP: World Records T 520/ST 520 LP: EMI SXDW 3049 CD: EMI CDM 769 5012
April 1958	Nordmo-Loevberg	LP: Columbia 33CX 1651/SAX 2353 LP: Angel 35715

Lohengrin, Excerpt (Euch Lüften, die mein Klagen)

May 1956	Schwarzkopf, G.Hoffman, Czerwenka	Columbia unpublished
April 1958	Nordmo-Loevberg	LP: Columbia 33CX 1651/SAX 2353 LP: Angel 35715

Tannhäuser, Excerpt (Dich teure Halle!)

April 1956	Schwarzkopf	LP: Columbia 33CX 1658/SAX 2300 LP: Columbia (France) 33FCX 821 LP: Angel 35806 LP: World Records T 520/ST 520 LP: EMI SXDW 3049 CD: EMI CDM 769 5012
April 1958	Nordmo-Loevberg	LP: Columbia 33CX 1651/SAX 2353 LP: Angel 35715

Tannhäuser, Excerpt (Allmächt'ge Jungfrau)

April 1956	Schwarzkopf	LP: Columbia 33CX 1658/SAX 2300 LP: Columbia (France) 33FCX 821 LP: Angel 35806 LP: World Records T 520/ST 520 LP: EMI SXDW 3049 CD: EMI CDM 769 5012
April 1958	Nordmo-Loevberg	LP: Columbia 33CX 1651/SAX 2353 LP: Angel 35715

Die Walküre, Excerpt (Du bist der Lenz)

April 1958	Nordmo-Loevberg	LP: Columbia 33CX 1651/SAX 2353 LP: Angel 35715

CARL MARIA VON WEBER (1786-1926)

Der Beherrscher der Geister, Overture

March 1946   78: Columbia DX 1262

Der Freischütz, Overture

March 1946   78: Columbia DX 1244

Der Freischütz, Excerpt (Leise, leise)

May 1948	Welitsch	78: Columbia LX 1090 78: Columbia (USA) 72777D LP: Columbia (USA) ML 2139 LP: EMI HLM 7006/100 2671/1C047 01267M LP: World Records SH 289 LP: Angel 60202 CD: EMI CDH 761 0072
April 1956	Schwarzkopf	LP: Columbia 33CX 1658/SAX 2300 LP: Columbia (France) 33FCX 821 LP: Angel 35806 LP: World Records T 520/ST 520 LP: EMI SXDW 3049 CD: EMI CDM 769 5012/CDM 565 5772

Susskind

Der Freischütz, Excerpt (Und ob die Wolke)

| March 1953 | Hammond | LP: HMV ALP 1076 |
| April 1956 | Schwarzkopf | LP: Columbia 33CX 1658/SAX 2300
LP: Columbia (France) 33FCX 821
LP: Angel 35806/3754
LP: World Records T 520/ST 520
LP: EMI SXDW 3049
CD: EMI CDM 769 5012 |

Oberon, Overture

June 1947   Columbia unpublished

Oberon, Excerpt (Ozean, du Ungeheuer!)

April 1956   Schwarzkopf   Columbia unpublished

HUGO WOLF (1860-1903)

Italian Serenade

July 1945   78: Columbia DX 1236
<u>First published recording by Philharmonia Orchestra, on which it was described as Philharmonia String Orchestra</u>

Selected Records For Your Enjoyment

PAUL KLETZKI and the PHILHARMONIA ORCHESTRA

Serenade in C — *Tchaikovsky;*
"The Bartered Bride" — Overture — *Smetana;* **Bolero** — *Ravel* 33CX1164
"A Midsummer Night's Dream" — Incidental Music — *Mendelssohn*
33CX1174

IGOR MARKEVITCH and the PHILHARMONIA ORCHESTRA
Young Person's Guide to the Orchestra
(Variations and Fugue on a theme of Purcell) —
Britten (Narrator: Peter Pears)
Le Carnaval des Animaux — *Saint-Saëns*
(*Pianos:* GEZA ANDA and BELA SIKI) 33CX1175

HERBERT VON KARAJAN and the PHILHARMONIA ORCHESTRA
Sinfonia Concertante, K.297b — *Mozart;*
Eine kleine Nachtmusik, K.525 — *Mozart* 33CX1178
Symphony No. 3 in E flat ("Eroica") — *Beethoven* 33CX1046
Symphony No. 5 in E flat — *Sibelius;*
Finlandia — Symphonic Poem — *Sibelius* 33CX1047

ISSAY DOBROWEN and the PHILHARMONIA ORCHESTRA
Scheherazade — Symphonic Suite — *Rimsky-Korsakov* 33SX1007

GEZA ANDA and the PHILHARMONIA ORCHESTRA
conducted by ALCEO GALLIERA
Concerto No. 2 in C minor — *Rachmaninov;*
Solos: **Preludes in G, G minor** — *Rachmaninov* 33CX1143

DINU LIPATTI and the PHILHARMONIA ORCHESTRA
conducted by ALCEO GALLIERA
Concerto in A minor — *Grieg* 33C1040

DR. ALBERT SCHWEITZER
at the Organ of the Parish Church, Günsbach, Alsace
Fugue in A minor;
Fantasia and Fugue in G minor ("Great");
Toccata, Adagio and Fugue in C — *J. S. Bach* 33CX1074

COLUMBIA

33⅓ R.P.M. LONG PLAYING RECORDS

COLUMBIA GRAPHOPHONE COMPANY LIMITED, RECORD DIVISION, 8-11 GREAT CASTLE STREET LONDON, W.1

Paul Kletzki
1900-1973

PHILHARMONIA ORCHESTRA

Records by
PAUL KLETZKI
AND THE
PHILHARMONIA ORCHESTRA

BERLIOZ Overtures
Le carnaval romain, Béatrice et Bénédict,
Le Corsaire, Benvenuto Cellini, Les Francs juges
XLP30014

MENDELSSOHN A Midsummer Night's Dream
Incidental Music
with Adrienne Cole, Eileen McLoughlin & Chorus
XLP30025

PROKOFIEV Symphony No. 5 in B flat
ASD578   ALP2029

RIMSKY-KORSAKOV Scheherazade
with Hugh Bean, *violin*
SXLP20026   XLP20026

SCHUBERT Rosamunde, excerpts
XLP30041

SIBELIUS Symphony No. 1 in E minor
33CX1311

TCHAIKOVSKY Symphony No. 6 in B minor "Pathétique"
SXLP20027   XLP20027

TCHAIKOVSKY Manfred Symphony
XLP30015

ROYAL PHILHARMONIC ORCHESTRA
SCHUBERT Symphony No. 8 in B minor "Unfinished"
Rosamunde, excerpts
ASD296   ALP1725

TCHAIKOVSKY Francesca da Rimini;
Philharmonia Orchestra/Robert Irving
Tchaikovsky Hamlet—Fantasy Overture
XLP30036

Even if you don't collect records you'll find plenty to interest you each month in EMI's bright classical magazine RECORD TIMES—price one penny from record shops

EMI Records (The Gramophone Co. Ltd.). EMI House, 20 Manchester Sq., London W1

SAMUEL BARBER (1910-1981)

Adagio for strings

June 1953   78: Columbia LX 1595

LUDWIG VAN BEETHOVEN (1770-1827)

Violin Romances Nos. 1 and 2

December   Martzy   LP: Columbia 33CX 1497
1955

Coriolan Overture

October 1947   Columbia unpublished

Leonore No 3 Overture

October 1947   78: Columbia LX 1069-1070
                                    78: Columbia (France) LFX 816-817
                                    78: HMV (France) SL 150

ALBAN BERG (1885-1935)

Violin Concerto

August   Gertler   LP: Columbia 33C 1030
1953   LP: Columbia (Germany) C 70090

80 Kletzki

HECTOR BERLIOZ (1803-1869)

Béatrice et Bénédict, Overture

September 1951

78: Columbia LX 1529
78: Columbia (Italy) GQX 11524
78: Columbia (Australia) LOX 818
45: Columbia SEL 1502
45: Columbia (Italy) SEBQ 103
45: Columbia (Japan) EW 29
LP: Columbia 33CX 1003
LP: Columbia (France) 33FCX 173
LP: Columbia (Italy) 33QCX 10027
LP: Columbia (USA) RL 3071
LP: EMI XLP 30014

Benvenuto Cellini, Overture

September 1951

78: Columbia LX 8935-8936
45: Columbia SEL 1502
LP: Columbia 33CX 1003
LP: Columbia (France) 33FCX 173
LP: Columbia (Italy) 33QCX 10027
LP: Columbia (USA) RL 3071
LP: EMI XLP 30014

Le carnaval romain, Overture

July 1952

78: Columbia LX 1574
LP: EMI XLP 30014

Le corsair, Overture

September 1951

78: Columbia LX 1533
78: Columbia (Italy) GQX 16654
45: HMV 7P 354
LP: Columbia 33CX 1003
LP: Columbia (France) 33FCX 173
LP: Columbia (Italy) 33QCX 10027
LP: Columbia (USA) RL 3071
LP: EMI XLP 30014

Les francs juges, Overture

September 1951   78: Columbia LX 8926-8927
                                   LP: Columbia 33CX 1003
                                   LP: Columbia (France) 33FCX 173
                                   LP: Columbia (Italy) 33QCX 10027
                                   LP: Columbia (USA) RL 3071
                                   LP: EMI XLP 30014

GEORGES BIZET (1838-1875)

L'Arlésienne, Suite No 1

July 1952   Columbia unpublished

ERNEST BLOCH (1880-1959)

Violin Concerto

June 1963   Menuhin   LP: HMV ALP 2035/ASD 584
                                   LP: EMI XLP 30177/SXLP 30177/EX 29 08643

ALEXANDER BORODIN (1833-1887)

Symphony No 2

February 1954   LP: Columbia 33CX 1167
                                   CD: Testament SBT 1048

JOHANNES BRAHMS (1833-1897)

Violin Concerto

February 1954	Martzy	LP: Columbia 33CX 1165
		LP: Columbia (Italy) 33QCX 10102
		LP: Angel 35137
		CD: Testament SBT 1037

Double Concerto

June 1962	Ferras, Tortelier	LP: HMV ALP 1999/ASD 549
		LP: World Records T 699/ST 699
		LP: EMI SLS 27 00013

Haydn Variations

August 1958	LP: HMV ALP 1696

Tragic Overture

October 1947	78: Columbia LX 1251-1252
	LP: Columbia (USA) RL 3060

Hungarian Dance No 1

September 1951	78: Columbia LX 8926
	45: Columbia SEL 1510
	45: Columbia (Japan) EW 57

Hungarian Dance No 2

September 1951	78: Columbia LX 8935
	45: Columbia SEL 1510
	45: Columbia (Japan) EW 57

Hungarian Dance No 3

September 1951   78: Columbia LX 8935
                              45: Columbia SEL 1510
                              45: Columbia (Japan) EW 57

Hungarian Dance No 5

May 1948   78: Columbia LX 1252
                              LP: Columbia (USA) RL 3091

Hungarian Dance No 6

May 1948   78: Columbia LX 1252
                              LP: Columbia (USA) RL 3091

FREDERIC CHOPIN (1810-1849)

Piano Concerto No 1

April   Pollini   LP: HMV ALP 1794/ASD 370
1960   LP: Electrola E 80592/STE 80592
                              LP: EMI XLP 30160/SXLP 30160
                              CD: EMI CDM 764 3542/CDM 769 0042

Piano Concerto No 2

November   Malcuzynski   78: Columbia LX 1013-1016/LX 8571-8574
1946   78: Columbia (France) LFX 790-793
                              78: Columbia (Italy) GQX 11202-11205
                              78: Columbia (Austria) LVX 121-124
                              78: Columbia (Switzerland)LZX 211-214
                              78: Columbia (USA) M 776
                              LP: Columbia (USA) ML 4135

February-   Malcuzynski   LP: Columbia 33CX 1066
March 1953   LP: Columbia (France) 33FCX 154
                              LP: Angel 35030

Kletzki   84

MIKHAIL GLINKA (1804-1857)

Jota aragonesa

September   45: HMV 7ER 5153/RES 4259
1958   LP: HMV ALP 1679/ASD 343
                             LP: Angel 35766
                             LP: EMI CFP 40083
                             CD: EMI CZS 767 7262

Kamarinskaya

January 1955   45: Columbia SEL 1603

Russlan and Ludmila, Overture

September 1951   78: Columbia LX 8951
                             78: Columbia (Italy) GQX 8047

FERDINAND HEROLD (1791-1833)

Zampa, Overture

January 1955   45: Columbia SEL 1541

MIKHAIL IPPOLITOV-IVANOV (1859-1935)

Caucasian Sketches

June 1953   LP: Columbia 33CX 1167

GUSTAV MAHLER (1860-1911)

Symphony No 4

April- June 1957	Loose	LP: Columbia 33CX 1541/SAX 2345 LP: Columbia (Germany) C 90965 LP: Angel 35570 LP: EMI XLP 30054/SXLP 30054 CD: EMI CZS 767 7262

Adagietto (Symphony No 5)

October 1959	LP: HMV ALP 1774/ASD 352 LP: Angel 3607 CD: EMI CZS 767 7262

Das Lied von der Erde

October 1959	Dickie, Fischer-Dieskau	LP: HMV ALP 1773-1774/ASD 351-352 LP: Angel 3607 LP: EMI XLP 30165/SXLP 30165/EMX 4120731 CD: EMI CZS 762 7072

FELIX MENDELSSOHN-BARTHOLDY

Violin Concerto

December 1955	Martzy	LP: Columbia 33CX 1497 LP: Angel 35236 CD: Testament SBT 1037

A Midsummer Night's Dream, Incidental music

February 1954	Cole, McLoughlin BBC Chorus	LP: Columbia 33CX 1174 LP: EMI XLP 30025 Excerpts 78: Columbia LX 1615 45: Columbia SEL 1534 LP: EMI RLS 7701

Kletzki   86

Hebrides, Overture

March 1954   Columbia unpublished

Die Heimkehr aus der Fremde, Overture

March 1954   45: Columbia SEL 1525

Ruy Blas, Overture

March 1954   45: Columbia SEL 1525

MODEST MUSSORGSKY (1839-1881)

Khovantschina, Dance of the Persian Slaves

January 1955   45: Columbia SEL 1542

Night on Bare Mountain

September 1951   78: Columbia LX 8951-8952
                                    78: Columbia (Italy) GQX 8047-8048

OTTO NICOLAI (1810-1849)

Die lustigen Weiber von Windsor, Overture

January 1955   45: Columbia SEL 1541

SERGEI PROKOFIEV (1891-1953)

Symphony No 5

June 1963   LP: HMV ALP 2029/ASD 578
                                    LP: Electrola E 91330/STE 91330
                                    LP: EMI CFP 200

SERGEI RACHMANINOV (1873-1943)

Piano Concerto No 3

April 1949	Malcuzynski	78: Columbia LX 1352-1356/LX 8767-8771 78: Columbia (Austria) LVX 116-120 LP: Columbia 33CX 1161 LP: Columbia (France) 33FCX 104 LP: Columbia (USA) ML 54369

MAURICE RAVEL (1875-1937)

Bolero

June 1953   LP: Columbia 33CX 1164
                     LP: EMI MFP 2045

Pavane pour une infante défunte

June 1953   45: Columbia SEL 1524

NIKOLAI RIMSKY-KORSAKOV (1844-1908)

Scheherazade

April 1960   LP: EMI XLP 20026/SXLP 20026/CFP 40341
                     CD: EMI CDCFP 4341/CDB 767 4782

Tsar Sultan, Suite

August-   LP: HMV ALP 1679/ASD 343
September 1958   LP: Angel 35766
                     LP: EMI CFP 40083
                     CD: EMI CZS 568 0982/CZS 767 7262
                         CDCFP 5006/CDB 569 5502

PHILHARMONIA CO[N

(Artistic Director :

SEASON

Monday, April 8th, at 8 p.m.

DIETRICH FISCHER-DIESKAU

GERALD MOORE

SCHUBERT RECITAL

7/6   5/-
ALL OTHER SEATS SOLD

Friday, May 3rd, at 8 p.m.

PHILHARMONIA
ORCHESTRA

RUDOLF KEMPE
AASE NORDMO-LOVBERG
(First appearance in London)

Haydn: Symphony No. 73 in D, "The Hunt"
Wagner: "Tristan": Prelude and Liebestod
Beethoven: "Fidelio": Abscheulicher!
Dvorak: Symphony No. 5 in E minor, Op. 95, "From the New World"

15/-,   12/6,   10/6,   7/6,   5/-
Booking opens April 3rd

TICKETS from ROYAL FESTIVAL HALL (WATerloo 3191), IBBS & TI[L

NCERT SOCIETY LTD.
(WALTER LEGGE)
1956 - 57

Tuesday, June 4th, at 8 p.m.

PHILHARMONIA
ORCHESTRA

THURSTON DART
ELISABETH SCHWARZKOPF

BACH
Programme to be announced

| 15/- | 12/6 | 10/6 | 7/6 | 5/- |

Booking opens May 4th

Friday, June 7th, at 8 p.m.

PHILHARMONIA
ORCHESTRA

PAUL KLETZKI
GEZA ANDA

TCHAIKOVSKY
Fantasy Overture — Romeo and Juliet
Piano Concerto No. 1 in B flat, Op. 23
Symphony No. 5 in E minor, Op. 64

| 15/- | 12/6 | 10/6 | 7/6 | 5/- |

Booking opens May 7th

LETT LTD., 124 Wigmore Street, W.1 (WELbeck 8418) and usual agencies

Kletzki

ARTUR SCHNABEL (1882-1951)

Rhapsody for orchestra

April 1950　　　　　　　　　　78: Columbia LX 8843-8844

FRANZ SCHUBERT (1797-1828)

Symphony No 8 "Unfinished"

November 1946　　　　　　　　78: Columbia LX 1222-1224/LX 8690-8692
　　　　　　　　　　　　　　　78: Columbia (Switzerland)LZX 219-221
　　　　　　　　　　　　　　　78: International Columbia
　　　　　　　　　　　　　　　　　LCX 128-130

Rosamunde, Incidental music

July 1952　　　　　　　　　　LP: Columbia 33CX 1157
　　　　　　　　　　　　　　　LP: EMI XLP 30041
　　　　　　　　　　　　　　　<u>Excerpt from Overture</u>
　　　　　　　　　　　　　　　LP: Columbia 33SX 1394

JEAN SIBELIUS (1865-1957)

Symphony No 1

July 1955

LP: Columbia 33CX 1311
LP: Columbia (Germany) C 90472
LP: Columbia (Italy) 33QCX 10204
LP: Columbia (Japan) XL 5186
LP: Angel 35313
CD: Testament SBT 1049

Symphony No 2

July 1955

LP: Columbia 33CX 1332/SAX 2280
LP: Columbia (Italy) 33QCX 10228
LP: Columbia (Japan) XL 5146
LP: Angel 35314
LP: EMI XLP 30061/SXLP 30061
CD: EMI CZS 767 7262

Symphony No 3

July 1955

LP: Columbia (Japan) XL 5152
LP: Angel 35315
CD: Testament SBT 1049

En Saga

May 1948

78: Columbia LX 1307-1309/LX 8729-8731
78: Columbia (Italy) GQX 11423-11425

July 1955

Columbia unpublished

Valse triste

May 1948

78: Columbia LX 1309
LP: Columbia (USA) RL 3091

Kletzki

BEDRICH SMETANA (1824-1884)

The Bartered Bride, Overture

June 1953 78: Columbia LX 1594
 45: Columbia SEL 1510
 LP: Columbia 33CX 1164
 LP: EMI MFP 2045

JOSEF STRAUSS (1827-1870)

Sphärenklänge, Waltz

January 1955 45: Columbia SEL 1535

FRANZ VON SUPPE (1819-1895)

Beautiful Galatea, Overture

January 1955 45: Columbia SEL 1603

Light Cavalry, Overture

January 1955 45: Columbia SEL 1529

Morning Noon and Night in Vienna, Overture

January 1955 45: Columbia SEL 1529

Pique Dame, Overture

January 1955 45: Columbia SEL 1542

PIOTR TCHAIKOVSKY (1840-1893)

Symphony No 5

November 1946
78: Columbia LX 969-974/LX 8541-8546
78: Columbia (France) LFX 752-757
78: Columbia (Italy) GQX 11196-11201
78: Columbia (USA) M 701
LP: Columbia (USA) RL 3036

Symphony No 6 "Pathétique"

April 1960
LP: EMI XLP 20027/SXLP 20027/CFP 40220/ CFP 41 44521
CD: EMI CDCFP 5006/CDB 569 5502

Manfred Symphony

January-
February 1954
LP: Columbia 33CX 1189
LP: EMI XLP 30015
CD: Testament SBT 1048

Serenade for strings

July 1952
LP: Columbia 33CX 1164
LP: EMI MFP 2045
<u>Waltz</u>
45: Columbia SEL 1535

94   Kletzki

Capriccio italien

April 1950

78: Columbia LX 8736-8737
78: Columbia (Italy) GQX 11459-11460
78: Columbia (USA) M 15161-15162

September 1958

LP: HMV ALP 1679/ASD 343
LP: Angel 35766
LP: EMI CFP 40083/CFP 40341
CD: EMI CDCFP 4341/CDB 767 4782

Andante cantabile (String Quartet in D), arranged by Schmid

September 1958

45: HMV 7ER 5153/RES 4259
LP: HMV ALP 1679/ASD 343
LP: Angel 35766
LP: EMI CFP 40083
CD: EMI CZS 767 7262

RICHARD WAGNER (1813-1883)

Der fliegende Holländer, Overture

October 1947

78: Columbia LX 1160-1161
78: Columbia (France) LFX 867-868
78: Columbia (Italy) QCX 11305-11306
78: Columbia (Austria) LVX 108-109
78: Columbia (Switzerland)LZX 258-259
LP: Columbia (USA) RL 3060

Lohengrin, Prelude

October 1947

78: Columbia LX 1153
78: Columbia (Italy) GQX 11269
LP: Columbia (USA) RL 3060

Lohengrin, Act 3 Prelude

October 1947
78: Columbia LX 1161
78: Columbia (France) LFX 868
78: Columbia (Italy) GQX 11306
78: Columbia (Switzerland) LZX 259
LP: Columbia (USA) RL 3060

Siegfried Idyll

May 1948
78: Columbia LX 1296-1297
78: Columbia (Italy) GQX 11414-11415

August 1958
LP: HMV ALP 1696

Tannhäuser, Overture and Venusberg Music

June 1953
LP: Columbia 33CX 1129

Träume (Wesendonk-Lieder), arrangement

August-
September
1958
Bean
LP: HMV ALP 1696

Tristan und Isolde, Prelude and Liebestod

June 1953
LP: Columbia 33CX 1129

JAROMIR WEINBERGER (1896-1967)

Schwanda the Bagpiper, Polka and Fugue

January 1955
Columbia unpublished

Nicolai Malko
1888-1961

PHILHARMONIA
ORCHESTRA

new LPs for the new year

NICOLAI MALKO
THE PHILHARMONIA ORCHESTRA
Beethoven Overtures: "Leonora", No. 3, "Coriolan",
"Die Geschöpfe des Prometheus"
DLP 1061

CHARLES MÜNCH
BOSTON SYMPHONY ORCHESTRA *with*
GREGOR PIATIGORSKY *(Cello)* RICHARD BURGIN *(Violin)*
JOSEPH DE PASQUALE *(Viola)*
Don Quixote: Richard Strauss
(Fantastic Variations on a Knightly Theme)
ALP 1211

STOKOWSKI
AND HIS SYMPHONY ORCHESTRA
Symphony No. 1 in E Minor: Sibelius
ALP 1210

"HIS MASTER'S VOICE"
Long Play 33⅓ R.P.M. RECORDS

THE GRAMOPHONE COMPANY LIMITED (RECORD DIVISION) 8-11 GREAT CASTLE STREET LONDON · W

LUDWIG VAN BEETHOVEN (1770-1827)

Coriolan, Overture

January 1953   78: HMV C 4232
                                78: HMV (Austria) GB 83
                                LP: HMV DLP 1061
                                LP: HMV (France) FFLP 1047
                                LP: HMV (Italy) QDLP 6022
                                LP: Victor LBC 1087

Die Geschöpfe des Prometheus, Overture

January 1953   LP: HMV DLP 1061
                                LP: HMV (France) FFLP 1047
                                LP: HMV (Italy) QDLP 6022
                                LP: Victor LBC 1087

Leonore No 3, Overture

January 1953   45: HMV 7EP 7062
                                LP: HMV DLP 1061
                                LP: HMV (France) FFLP 1047
                                LP: HMV (Italy) QDLP 6022
                                LP: Victor LBC 1087

LUIGI BOCCHERINI (1743-1805)

Minuetto (Quintet in E), arrangement

May 1953   45: HMV 7EP 7067

ARRIGO BOITO (1842-1918)

Mefistofele, Excerpt (Son lo spirito che nega)

December   Christoff   78: HMV DB 21047
1949   45: HMV (France) 7RF 263
                                LP: EMI RLS 735/1C 147 03336-03337M
                                CD: EMI CDH 565 5002

ALEXANDER BORODIN (1833-1887)

Symphony No 2

February-　　　　　　　　　　78: HMV C 3971-3974/C 7781-7784
March 1948　　　　　　　　　45: Victor WBC 1024
　　　　　　　　　　　　　　　LP: Victor LBC 1024

September　　　　　　　　　 LP: HMV CLP 1075
1955　　　　　　　　　　　　 LP: EMI XLP 30010

Symphony No 3, arranged by Glazunov

September　　　　　　　　　 LP: HMV CLP 1075
1955　　　　　　　　　　　　 LP: EMI XLP 30010
　　　　　　　　　　　　　　　CD: Testament SBT 1062

Prince Igor, Overture

February　　　　　　　　　　 LP: HMV CLP 1110
1956　　　　　　　　　　　　 LP: Angel HC 1020
　　　　　　　　　　　　　　　CD: Testament SBT 1062

Prince Igor, Polovtsian March and Polovtsian Dances

January 1953　　　　　　　　LP: HMV DLP 1092
　　　　　　　　　　　　　　　CD: Testament SBT 1062

LEO DELIBES (1836-1891)

La Source, Pas de Naila

May 1953　　　　　　　　　　 78: HMV C 4261
　　　　　　　　　　　　　　　45: HMV 7P 152
　　　　　　　　　　　　　　　LP: Victor LBC 1080

ANTONIN DVORAK (1841-1904)

Symphony No 9 "From the New World"

February 1956　　　　　　　 LP: HMV CLP 1125
　　　　　　　　　　　　　　　LP: EMI MFP 2004

Slavonic Dances Op 46

April–　　　　　　　　LP: HMV CLP 1019
May 1953　　　　　　　LP: HMV (France) FALP 341
　　　　　　　　　　　LP: HMV (Italy) QCLP 12008
　　　　　　　　　　　LP: Victor LM 2096
　　　　　　　　　　　No 3 only
　　　　　　　　　　　45: HMV 7EP 7067

Slavonic Dances Op 72

April–　　　　　　　　LP: HMV CLP 1020
May 1953　　　　　　　LP: HMV (France) FALP 342
　　　　　　　　　　　LP: HMV (Italy) QCLP 12009
　　　　　　　　　　　LP: Victor LM 2107

ALEXANDER GLAZUNOV (1865-1936)

Les ruses d'amour, Excerpts from the ballet

December 1950　　　　78: HMV C 7875

The Seasons, Excerpts

March 1950　　　　　　78: HMV C 7874-7875
　　　　　　　　　　　45: Victor WBC 1022
　　　　　　　　　　　LP: Victor LBC 1022
　　　　　　　　　　　LP: HMV (France) FBLP 1004

Les vendredis, Polka arranged by Malko

May 1953　　　　　　　LP: HMV DLP 1092
　　　　　　　　　　　CD: Testament SBT 1062

Raymonda, Waltz

March 1950　　　　　　78: HMV C 3991
　　　　　　　　　　　45: Victor WBC 1022
　　　　　　　　　　　LP: Victor LBC 1022
　　　　　　　　　　　LP: HMV (France) FBLP 1004

REINHOLD GLIERE (1875-1956)

The Red Poppy, Russian Sailor's Dance

November 1948
78: HMV C 3828
45: HMV 7P 128
45: Electrola 7PW 104
45: HMV (France) 7BF 1019
45: Victor WBC 1026
LP: Victor LBC 1026
LP: HMV (France) FBLP 1004

MIKHAIL GLINKA (1804-1857)

Jota aragonesa

November 1948
78: HMV C 3878

Russlan and Ludmila, Overture

February 1956
LP: HMV CLP 1110
LP: Angel HC 1020

Russlan and Ludmila, Oriental Dances

December 1950-
January 1952
78: HMV C 4196

Valse-Fantaisie

November 1948
78: HMV C 3949
45: Victor WBC 1021
LP: Victor LBC 1021

CHARLES GOUNOD (1818-1893)

Judex, from the oratorio Mors et vita

May 1953
78: HMV C 4261
45: HMV 7P 152
LP: Victor LBC 1080

EDVARD GRIEG (1843-1907)

Lyric Suite

April-
May 1953
        LP: HMV CLP 1020
        LP: HMV (France) FALP 342
        LP: HMV (Italy) QCLP 12009
        LP: Victor LM 2107
        <u>Excerpt</u>
        45: HMV 7EP 7067

FRANZ JOSEF HAYDN (1732-1809)

Serenade (String Quartet in F), arrangement

May 1953
        45: HMV 7EP 7067

FERDINAND HEROLD (1791-1833)

Zampa, Overture

January
1953
        78: HMV C 4227
        78: HMV (Austria) GB 82
        78: HMV (Italy) S 10616
        LP: HMV DLP 1069
        LP: HMV (Italy) QDLP 6024
        LP: EMI MFP 2034

MIKHAIL IPPOLITOV-IVANOV (1859-1935)

Caucasian Sketches

November
1948
        78: HMV C 3936-3937
        45: Victor WBC 1019
        LP: Victor LBC 1019

ARAM KHACHATURIAN (1903-1978)

Gayaneh, Lullaby and Dance of the Maidens

March 1947
        78: HMV C 3572
        45: HMV 7P 103
        45: Electrola 7PW 123
        45: HMV (France) 7BF 1054

ANATOLE LIADOV (1855-1914)

Baba Yaga

February 1948	78: HMV C 3974

8 Russian Folksongs

May 1953	LP: HMV DLP 1092 LP: Angel 35594 CD: Testament SBT 1062 CD: EMI CZS 568 5502

FELIX MENDELSSOHN-BARTHOLDY (1809-1847)

Capriccio brillant for piano and orchestra

February 1953	Lympany	78: HMV C 4241 LP: HMV CLP 1007 LP: HMV (France) FELP 113 LP: HMV (Italy) QCLP 12003 LP: Victor LHMV 15

Bees' Wedding and Spring Song (Songs without Words), arrangement

May 1953	78: HMV C 4246 78: HMV (Italy) S 10618 45: HMV 7P 148 LP: Victor LBC 1080

Hebrides, Overture

February 1956	LP: HMV CLP 1110 LP: Angel HC 1020 LP: EMI MFP 2034

Ruy Blas, Overture

March 1956	LP: HMV CLP 1110 LP: Angel HC 1020 LP: EMI MFP 2034

WOLFGANG AMADEUS MOZART (1756-1791)

Piano Concerto No 12

April 1954	Lympany	LP: HMV CLP 1038

MODEST MUSSORGSKY (1839-1881)

Boris Godunov, Excerpt (Pimen's Monologue)

December 1949 Christoff
78: HMV DA 1938
45: HMV (France) 7RF 213
LP: EMI RLS 735/1C 147 03336-03337M
CD: EMI CDH 764 2522

Gopak (Sorochinsky Fair)

November 1948
78: HMV C 3828
45: HMV 7P 128
45: Electrola 7PW 104
45: HMV (France) 7BF 1019

Khovantschina, Entr'acte

January 1952
78: HMV C 7914
78: HMV (Austria) GB 72
45: HMV 7P 143
45: HMV (France) 7BF 1059
45: HMV (Italy) 7PQ 2019
45: Victor WBC 1022
LP: Victor LBC 1022

Night on Bare Mountain

January 1952
78: HMV C 7914-7915
45: Victor WBC 1022
LP: Victor LBC 1022

SERGEI PROKOFIEV (1891-1953)

Symphony No 1 "Classical"

February
1955

45: HMV 7EP 7072
LP: HMV CLP 1044
LP: Victor LM 2092
LP: HMV (Italy) QCLP 12016
LP: EMI SXLP 30437/CFP 4523
CD: EMI CDCFP 4523/CDB 762 7752

Symphony No 7

February
1955

LP: HMV CLP 1044
LP: Victor LM 2092
LP: HMV (Italy) QCLP 12016
LP: EMI SXLP 30437/CFP 4523
CD: EMI CDCFP 4523/CDB 762 7752
<u>First stereophonic recording undertaken by EMI, although not issued in this form until the 1980s</u>

The Love of 3 Oranges, Suite

February
1955

LP: HMV CLP 1060
LP: Angel 35594
LP: EMI MFP 2047/SXLP 30437/CFP 4523
CD: EMI CDCFP 4523/CDB 762 7752

SERGEI RACHMANINOV (1873-1943)

Piano Concerto No 1

April 1954   Lympany

LP: HMV CLP 1037
LP: HMV (France) FELP 123
LP: HMV (Italy) QCLP 12013
CD: Olympia OCD 190

Piano Concerto No 2

February
1953   Lympany

LP: HMV CLP 1007
LP: HMV (France) FELP 113
LP: HMV (Italy) QCLP 12003
LP: Victor LHMV 15
LP: EMI MFP 2035
CD: Olympia OCD 190

NIKOLAI RIMSKY-KORSAKOV (1844-1908)

Flight of the Bumble Bee (Tsar Saltan)

November
1948

78: HMV C 3828
45: HMV 7P 128
45: Electrola 7PW 104
45: HMV (France) 7BF 1019
45: Victor WBC 1026
LP: Victor LBC 1026

Ivan the Terrible, Overture

March 1956

LP: HMV CLP 1110
LP: Angel HC 1020
CD: Testament SBT 1062

The Snow Maiden, Cortège and Dance of the Tumblers

March 1956

LP: HMV CLP 1110
LP: Angel HC 1020

JEAN SIBELIUS (1865-1957)

Finlandia

February
1948

78: HMV C 3767
78: HMV (Finland) TH 30
45: HMV 7R 101
45: Electrola 7PW 117
45: Victor WBC 1028/ERAB 2
LP: Victor LBC 1028

FRANZ VON SUPPE (1819-1895)

Poet and Peasant, Overture

February
1956

LP: HMV CLP 1110
LP: Angel HC 1020
LP: EMI MFP 2034

SERGEI TANEYEV (1856-1915)

Suite de concert for violin and orchestra

| February 1956 | D.Oistrakh | LP: Columbia 33CX 1390
LP: Angel 35355
LP: EMI SLS 5004
CD: EMI CDM 565 4192 |

PIOTR TCHAIKOVSKY (1840-1893)

Symphony No 4

January 1953
- 45: Victor WBC 1052
- LP: HMV CLP 1045
- LP: HMV (Denmark) KBH 1016
- LP: HMV (France) FELP 129
- LP: Victor LBC 1052

Symphony No 6 "Pathétique"

March 1947
- 78: HMV C 3630-3635/C 7697-7702
- 45: Victor WBC 1002
- LP: Victor LBC 1002
- LP: HMV (France) FELP 139

Suite No 3, Theme and Variations

March 1950
- 78: HMV C 4058-4060/C 7826-7828
- 45: Victor WBC 1024
- LP: Victor LBC 1024

1812 Overture

March 1947
- 78: HMV C 3617-3618/DB 4274-4275
- 78: HMV (France) SL 119-120
- 45: Victor WBC 1014
- LP: Victor LBC 1014

February 1953
- LP: HMV DLP 1069
- LP: EMI MFP 2034

Casse Noisette, Suite

March 1947-   78: HMV C 3835-3837/C 7744-7746/DB 4276-8
February   78: HMV (France) SL 110-112
1948

February   45: HMV 7EP 7077/PES 5252
1955   LP: HMV CLP 1060
               LP: Angel 35594
               LP: EMI MFP 2047/ESD 7115
               Excerpt
               45: HMV 7P 205

The Sleeping Beauty, Rose Adagio and Puss in Boots

January   78: HMV C 4212
1952   78: HMV (Italy) S 10608
               45: HMV 7EP 7017
               45: HMV (Italy) 7EPQ 533

The Sleeping Beauty, Entry of Lilac Fairy and Bluebird Pas de Deux

January   78: HMV C 4205
1952   78: HMV (Italy) S 10612
               45: HMV 7EP 7017
               45: HMV (Italy) 7EPQ 533

The Sleeping Beauty, Dance of the Maids of Honour and Pas de caractère for Red Riding Hood

January   78: HMV C 4258
1952   78: HMV (Italy) S 10612
               45: HMV 7EP 7017
               45: HMV (Italy) 7EPQ 533

Victor LP LBC 1007 published as containing Malko's Sleeping Beauty Suite actually has a version conducted by Constant Lambert

110   Malko

Mazeppa, Gopak

March 1950   78: HMV C 3991
                                    45: HMV 7P 143

The Voyevode, Intermezzo

December   78: HMV C 4060/C 7826
1950

RICHARD WAGNER (1813-1883)

Der fliegende Holländer, Overture

January   78: HMV C 4176
1952   45: Victor WBC 1048
                                    LP: Victor LBC 1048

CARL MARIA VON WEBER (1786-1826)

Oberon, Overture

May 1953   78: HMV C 4240
                                    LP: HMV DLP 1069
                                    LP: HMV (Italy) QDLP 6024

7-inch Light Blue Label — 12/-
(PLUS 3/11d. TAX)

7-inch Dark Blue Label — 8/6
(PLUS 2/9½d. TAX)

7-inch Green Label — 7/-
(PLUS 2/3½d. TAX)

GEORGE WELDON
and the PHILHARMONIA ORCHESTRA
Variations 8 and 9 *(from " Enigma Variations ") — Elgar ;*
Pomp and Circumstance March No. 1 in D — *Elgar* SED5520
" Cavalleria Rusticana " — Intermezzo — *Mascagni (organ :* GERAINT JONES*)*
" The Sleeping Beauty " Waltz — *Tchaikovsky ;*

and the LONDON SYMPHONY ORCHESTRA
Andante Cantabile *(from Quartet No. 1 in D) — Tchaikovsky* . . . SED5518
Henry VIII Dances — *German ;*
Merrie England — Dances — *German* SED5515
Overture in D minor — *Handel arr. Elgar ;*
" Solomon " — Sinfonia : Arrival of the Queen of Sheba ;
" Occasional Oratorio " — March — *Handel*
SED5516

SIR MALCOLM SARGENT
and the LIVERPOOL PHILHARMONIA ORCHESTRA
with the HUDDERSFIELD CHORAL SOCIETY
(Chorus Master : HERBERT BARDGETT.
Organ : ERNEST COOPER*)*
" Messiah " Choruses — *Handel :*
Let us break their bonds asunder ;
Hallelujah ;
Worthy is the Lamb ;
Amen - SEL1512
And the Glory of the Lord ;
And He shall purify ;
Glory to God ;
For unto us a Child is Born - . SEL1519
with ELSIE MORISON
" Messiah " Arias — *Handel :*
I know that my Redeemer liveth ;
with MARJORIE THOMAS
He was despised - . . . SEL1513
Recit. Then shall the eyes ;
Air. He shall feed His flock (Come unto Him) ;
with MARJORIE THOMAS &
HUDDERSFIELD CHORAL SOCIETY
Recit. Behold a Virgin shall conceive ;
Air : O Thou that tellest . . SEL1520

ANDRÉ CLUYTENS
and FRENCH RADIO ORCHESTRA
" L'Arlésienne " — Suite No. 1 — *Bizet ;*
Prélude *(Saxophone Solo :* MARCEL MULE*) ;*
" L'Arlésienne " — Suite No. 2 — *Bizet ;*
Pastorale SEL1521

ALCEO GALLIERA
and the PHILHARMONIA ORCHESTRA
" Il Barbiere de Siviglia " — Overture — *Rossini ;*
" La Traviata " — Preludes to Acts 1 and 3 — *Verdi* SED5517

LOUIS KENTNER
Csardas Macabre — *Liszt ;*
En Reve (Nocturne) — *Liszt ;*
Richard Wagner (Venezia) — *Liszt* SED5519

JOAN HAMMOND
" Madama Butterfly " — *Puccini :*
One Fine Day ;
" Tosca " — *Puccini :* Love and Music ;
" La Bohème " — *Puccini :* They call me Mimi ;
" Gianni Schicchi " — *Puccini :*
O my beloved Daddy - . . SED5514

MARIA MENEGHINI CALLAS
and **ANNA MARIA CANALI**
" Lucia di Lammermoor " — Act 1 — *Donizetti ;*
Regnava nel Silenzio ; Quando Rapito ;

GIUSEPPE DI STEFANO
Act 3 — Tombe degl' avi miei ;
Fra poco a me ricovero - SEL1522

PAUL KLETZKI
and the PHILHARMONIA ORCHESTRA
Hungarian Dances — *Brahms ;*
No. 1 in G minor ; No. 2 in F major ;
No. 3 in F major ;
" Bartered Bride " — Overture — *Smetana*
SEL1510

GEZA ANDA
Valse lente — Paraphrase *(from " Coppélia ") Delibes, arr. Dohnányi ;*
Etude de Concert No. 3 in D flat — *Liszt*
SEL1516

ELISABETH SCHWARZKOPF
" Don Giovanni " - Act 2 — *Mozart ;*
Recit. and Aria : Non mi dir ;
" Idomeneo " — Act 3 — *Mozart ;*
Zeffiretti lusinghieri . . . SEL1515

DINU LIPATTI
Alborada del Gracioso *(Miroirs No. 4) — Ravel ;*
Sonetto del Petrarca No. 104 *(No. 5 of Deuxième Année " L'Italie) — Liszt* SEB3501

SIR THOMAS BEECHAM, Bart.
and the ROYAL PHILHARMONIC ORCHESTRA
Scènes historiques — *Sibelius ;*
Festivo ; At the Drawbridge - SEB3501

COLUMBIA
7 inch 45 R.P.M. EXTENDED PLAY RECORDS

COLUMBIA GRAPHOPHONE COMPANY LIMITED, RECORD DIVISION, 8-11 GREAT CASTLE STREET, LONDON, W.1

Issay Dobrowen
1891-1953

PHILHARMONIA ORCHESTRA

Superb recordings by the
PHILHARMONIA ORCHESTRA

Conducted by Otto Klemperer
BEETHOVEN: Symphony No. 2 in D
Coriolan Overture   Prometheus Overture
33CX 1615

Conducted by Herbert von Karajan
BIZET: L'Arlésienne Suites Nos. 1 and 2
Carmen Suite No. 1
33CX 1608
TCHAIKOVSKY: Symphony No. 6 in B minor ('Pathétique')
33CX 1377

Conducted by Thomas Schippers
TCHAIKOVSKY: Symphony No. 4 in F minor
33CX 1609

Conducted by Carlo Maria Giulini
FRANCK: Symphony in D minor
Psyché et Éros
33CX 1589

Conducted by Alceo Galliera
WAGNER: Siegfried Idyll
STRAUSS: Don Juan
33C 1060

The above are
COLUMBIA
Long Play 33⅓ R.P.M. records
E.M.I. Records Ltd., 8–11 Great Castle Street, London, W.1

Issay Dobrowen

LUDWIG VAN BEETHOVEN (1770-1827)

Symphony No 5

June 1946   HMV unpublished

Piano Concerto No 2

June 1946   Schnabel   78: HMV DB 6323-6326/C 9099-9102
                                   LP: HMV COLH 2
                                   LP: Electrola E 60620/WDLP 644/E 90192
                                   LP: Toshiba GR 4006/GR 2091
                                   LP: Angel 6043
                                   CD: Testament SBT 1020

Piano Concerto No 3

May 1947   Schnabel   LP: HMV COLH 3
                                   LP: Electrola E 60622/WDLP 645/E 90193
                                   LP: Toshiba GR 4006/GR 2004
                                   CD: Testament SBT 1021

Piano Concerto No 4

June 1946   Schnabel   78: HMV DB 6303-6306/DB 9032-9035
                                   LP: Victor LCT 1131/LVT 1131
                                   LP: HMV COLH 4
                                   LP: Electrola E 60623/WDLP 646/E 90194
                                   LP: Toshiba GR 4006/GR 2091
                                   CD: Testament SBT 1021

Leonore No 3 Overture

May 1947-   HMV unpublished
February 1948

HECTOR BERLIOZ (1803-1869)

Le carnaval romain, Overture

February 1948   78: HMV C 3709

ARRIGO BOITO (1842-1918)

Mefistofele, Excerpt (Ave signor!)

May 1949   Christoff   78: HMV DB 21047
                                 45: HMV (France) 7RF 263
                                 LP: EMI RLS 735/1C 147 03336-03337M
                                 CD: EMI CDH 565 5002

ALEXANDER BORODIN (1833-1887)

Prince Igor, Overture

May 1948   78: HMV C 3979-3980

Prince Igor, Polovtsian March

May 1949   78: HMV C 3980
                                 45: Victor WBC 1026
                                 LP: Victor LBC 1026

Prince Igor, Excerpt (I hate a dreary life)

May 1950   Christoff   78: HMV DB 21127
                                 78: Victor M 1436
                                 45: Victor WDM 1436
                                 45: HMV 7ER 5007/7R 150
                                 45: Electrola 7RW 134
                                 45: HMV (France) 7RF 163
                                 45: HMV (Italy) 7ERQ 107/7RQ 3033
                                 LP: HMV BLP 1003
                                 LP: Electrola E 70018/WBLP 1003
                                 LP: HMV (Italy) QBLP 5002
                                 LP: HMV (Japan) HN 1011
                                 LP: EMI RLS 735/1C 147 03336-03337M
                                 CD: EMI CDH 764 2522

Prince Igor, Excerpt (How are you, Prince?)

May 1950   Christoff   78: HMV DB 21262
                                 78: Victor M 1436
                                 45: Victor WDM 1436
                                 45: HMV 7ER 5007/7R 125
                                 45: Electrola 7RW 111
                                 45: HMV (France) 7ERF 132/7RF 164
                                 LP: HMV BLP 1003
                                 LP: Electrola E 70018/WBLP 1003
                                 LP: HMV (Italy) QBLP 5002
                                 LP: HMV (Japan) HN 1011
                                 LP: EMI RLS 735/1C 147 03336-03337M
                                 CD: EMI CDH 764 2522

JOHANNES BRAHMS (1833-1897)

Piano Concerto No 2

April-   Solomon   78: HMV C 3610-3615/C 7688-7693
May 1947   LP: EMI XLP 30093/SLS 5094/
                                     1C 147 03081-03082M
                                 LP: Turnabout THS 65071
                                 CD: Testament SBT 1042

Violin Concerto

August   Neveu   78: HMV DB 6415-6419/DB 9126-9130
1946   LP: HMV COLH 80
                                 LP: Toshiba GR 2045
                                 LP: EMI RLS 739/29 08241
                                 CD: EMI CDH 761 0112

GUSTAVE CHARPENTIER (1860-1950)

Louise, Excerpt (Depuis le jour)

May 1950   Schwarzkopf   LP: EMI RLS 763/154 6133

Dobrowen

ERNEST CHAUSSON (1855-1899)

Poème for violin and orchestra

August 1946	Neveu	LP: HMV ALP 1520

LP: HMV ALP 1520
LP: HMV (France) FJLP 5037
LP: HMV (Australia) OALP 7502
LP: Toshiba GR 2189
LP: EMI RLS 729/2C 051 03982

UMBERTO GIORDANO (1867-1948)

Andrea Chenier, Excerpt (Vicino a te)

May 1950   Hammond, Schock   78: HMV DB 21260
78: HMV (Australia) ED 1247
LP: EMI 1C 147 28963-28964M/29 12013
CD: EMI CZS 767 1832

EDVARD GRIEG (1843-1907)

Symphonic Dance No 1

July 1951   78: HMV C 4142
78: HMV (Norway) ZN 599
45: HMV (France) 7BF 1047

FRANZ JOSEF HAYDN (1732-1809)

Symphony No 104 "London"

June 1946
78: HMV C 3515-3517/C 7645-7647
78: HMV (Switzerland) FKX 122-124

ANATOLE LIADOV (1855-1914)

Berceuse (Russian Folksongs)

May 1947
78: HMV C 3754/C 7722
78: HMV (France) SL 109

PIETRO MASCAGNI (1863-1945)

L'amico Fritz, Excerpt (Suzel, buon dì!)

May 1950   Hammond, Schock
78: HMV DB 21098
LP: EMI 1C 147 28963-28964M/29 12013
CD: EMI CZS 767 1832

NIKOLAI MEDTNER (1880-1951)

Piano Concerto No 2

May 1947	Medtner	78: HMV DB 6559-6563/DB 9191-9195 LP: Melodiya M10 41171-41172 CD: Testament SBT 1027

Piano Concerto No 3

May 1947	Medtner	78: HMV DB 6718-6722/DB 9259-9263 LP: Melodiya M10 41173-41174/ D 06501-06502 CD: Testament SBT 1027

WOLFGANG AMADEUS MOZART (1756-1791)

Le nozze di Figaro, Overture

July 1951	HMV unpublished

MODEST MUSSORGSKY (1839-1881)

Boris Godunov, Excerpt (Coronation Scene)

May 1949	Christoff	78: HMV DB 6948 78: Victor M 1436 45: Victor EHA 11 LP: Electrola WBLP 1008 LP: HMV (Australia) OBLP 5002 LP: HMV (Japan) HB 1010 LP: EMI RLS 735/1C 147 03336-03337M CD: EMI CDH 764 2522

Boris Godunov, Excerpt (Farewell and Prayer)

May 1949   Christoff   78: HMV DB 6935
                                     78: Victor M 1436
                                     45: HMV 7R 114
                                     45: Electrola 7RW 135
                                     LP: HMV BLP 1003
                                     LP: Electrola E 70018/WBLP 1003
                                     LP: HMV (Japan) HB 1010
                                     LP: EMI RLS 735/1C 147 03336-03337M
                                     CD: EMI CDH 764 2522

Boris Godunov, Excerpt (Death of Boris)

May 1949   Schwarzkopf,   78: HMV DB 21097
                  Christoff,   45: Victor ERA 11
                  Covent Garden   45: Electrola 7RW 135
                  Chorus   LP: HMV BLP 1003
                                     LP: Electrola E 70018/WBLP 1003
                                     LP: HMV (Australia) OBLP 5002
                                     LP: HMV (Japan) HB 1010
                                     LP: EMI RLS 735/1C 147 03336-03337M
                                     CD: EMI CDH 764 2522

Khovantschina, Excerpt (Here on this spot)

May 1950   Christoff   78: HMV DB 21207
                                     45: HMV 7ER 5007/7R 136
                                     45: Victor WHMV 1033
                                     45: HMV (France) 7ERF 132/7RF 165
                                     45: HMV (Italy) 7ERQ 107
                                     LP: Victor LHMV 1033
                                     LP: HMV (Japan) HN 1011
                                     LP: EMI RLS 735/1C 147 03336-03337M
                                     CD: EMI CDH 764 2522

Khovantschina, Prelude

September-   HMV unpublished
October 1947

Dobrowen

Khovantschina, Dance of the Persian Slaves

June 1946   HMV unpublished

Song of the Flea

October   Christoff   78: HMV DB 21305
1950   LP: EMI RLS 735/1C 147 03336-03337M
                                    CD: EMI CDH 764 2522

GIACOMO PUCCINI (1858-1924)

La Bohème, Excerpt (Donde lieta uscì)

May 1950   Schwarzkopf   Columbia unpublished

NIKOLAI RIMSKY-KORSAKOV (1844-1908)

Scheherazade

December 1952-   LP: Columbia 33SX 1007
January 1953   LP: Columbia (France) 33FCX 268/
                                       33FCX 30207
                                   LP: Columbia (Austria) 33VSX 501
                                   LP: Columbia (Italy) 33QCX 10021
                                   LP: Columbia (Spain) LALP 234
                                   LP: Angel 35009

Le coq d'or, Suite

December 1952   LP: Columbia 33SX 1010
                                   LP: Columbia (France) 33FCX 207
                                   LP: Columbia (Italy) 33QCX 207/QIMX 7016
                                   LP: Angel 35010
                                   LP: EMI XLP 30003
                                   <u>Excerpts</u>
                                   45: Columbia SED 5551

The Prophet, Song

October   Christoff   LP: EMI RLS 735
1950

Russian Easter Festival Overture

October   78: HMV C 7916-7917
1950   78: HMV (Italy) S 7000-7001

Sadko, Excerpt (Song of the Viking Guest)

May   Christoff   78: HMV DB 21127
1950   45: HMV 7R 150
                                        LP: EMI RLS 735/1C 147 03336-03337M
                                        CD: EMI CDH 764 2522

Tsar Sultan, Suite

December   LP: Columbia 33SX 1010
1952   LP: Columbia (France) 33FCX 207
                                        LP: Columbia (Italy) 33QCX 207/QIMX 7016
                                        LP: Angel 35010
                                        LP: EMI XLP 30003
                                        <u>Excerpts</u>
                                        45: Columbia SED 5551

CAMILLE SAINT-SAENS (1835-1921)

Samson et Dalila, Bacchanale

December 1952   78: Columbia DX 1898

ALEXANDER SCRIABIN (1872-1915)

Piano Concerto

May 1949   Solomon   CD: EMI CDH 763 8212

Dobrowen

PIOTR TCHAIKOVSKY (1840-1893)

Symphony No 4

June 1946-
February 1948

78: HMV C 3809-3813/C 7736-7740
78: HMV (Italy) S 10546-10550

Piano Concerto No 1

May 1949   Solomon

78: HMV C 3996-3999/C 7776-7779
78: Electrola EH 1365-1368
78: HMV (Italy) S 10578-10581
45: Victor WHMV 1028
LP: HMV CLP 1001
LP: Victor LHMV 1028
LP: Electrola WCLP 1001
LP: HMV (Australia) OCLP 12004
LP: HMV (Japan) HC 1002
LP: EMI SLS 5094/1C 053 01412M
CD: EMI CHS 764 8552
<u>Excerpt</u>
45: HMV 7P 200

Evgeny Onegin, Polonaise and Waltz

July 1951

78: HMV C 4190
CD: EMI CHS 764 8552

Serenade for strings

May 1947

78: HMV C 3751-3754/C 7722-7725
78: HMV (France) SL 106-109
45: Victor WBC 1021
LP: Victor LBC 1021

GIUSEPPE VERDI (1813-1901)

Aida, Excerpt (Ritorna vincitor!)

| July 1951 | Martinis | 78: Columbia LX 1536 |
| | | LP: Preiser PR 9855 |

Aida, Excerpt (O patria mia)

July 1951	Martinis	78: Columbia LX 1463
		78: Columbia (Italy) GQX 11512
		LP: Preiser PR 9855

Un ballo in maschera, Excerpt (Ecco l'orrido campo!)

July 1951	Martinis	78: Columbia LX 1548
		78: Columbia (Italy) GQX 11519
		LP: Preiser PR 9855

Don Carlo, Excerpt (Ella giammai m'amò)

| May 1949 | Christoff | HMV unpublished |

La forza del destino, Excerpt (Pace, pace, mio Dio!)

| July 1951 | Martinis | LP: Preiser PR 9855 |

Otello, Excerpt (Mia madre aveva una povera ancella)

| July 1951 | Martinis | 78: Columbia LX 1520 |
| | | LP: Preiser PR 9855 |

Otello, Excerpt (Ave Maria)

July 1951	Martinis	78: Columbia LX 1463
		78: Columbia (Italy) GQX 11512
		LP: Preiser PR 9855

Dobrowen

RICHARD WAGNER (1813-1883)

Lohengrin, Excerpt (Mein Herr und Gott!)

July 1951   Weber   Columbia unpublished

Die Meistersinger von Nürnberg, Overture

May 1947   78: HMV C 3926-3927
                                     45: Victor WBC 1048
                                     LP: Victor LBC 1048

Parsifal, Excerpt (Titurel, der fromme Held)

July 1951   Weber   78: Columbia LX 1441
                                     LP: EMI 1C 177 00933-00934M

Parsifal, Excerpt (O Gnade! Höchstes Heil!)

July 1951   Weber   78: Columbia LX 1442
                                     LP: EMI 1C 177 00933-00934M

Tannhäuser, Entry of the Guests

May 1949   78: HMV C 3927
                                     45: HMV 7P 140
                                     45: Electrola 7PW 126

Tannhäuser, Excerpt (Allmächt'ge Jungfrau!)

April   Flagstad   78: HMV DB 6795
1948   78: Victor 12-1062
                                     45: Victor 49-0783
                                     LP: EMI 1C 147 01491-01492M/EX 29 12273/
                                         29 10373/29 02123
                                     CD: EMI CDH 763 0302/CMS 764 0082

Tannhäuser, Excerpt (Gar viel und schön)

July 1951   Weber   78: Columbia (Germany) LWX 449
                                      LP: EMI 1C 177 00933-00934M/EX 769 7411
                                      CD: EMI CHS 769 7412

Tristan und Isolde, Prelude and Liebestod

September-   78: HMV C 4111-4113/C 7868-7870
October 1950

Tristan und Isolde, Excerpt (Narration and Curse)

March 1948   Flagstad,   78: HMV DB 6748-6749
                   Höngen   78: Victor M 1435
                                      45: Victor WDM 1435
                                      LP: Victor LM 1151
                                      LP: Electrola E 60619/WDLP 643
                                      LP: Angel 60082/6158
                                      LP: Toshiba GR 2192
                                      LP: EMI HQM 1138/1C 147 01491-01492M/
                                          EX 29 12273/29 10373
                                      CD: EMI CDH 763 0302

Tristan und Isolde, Excerpt (Liebestod)

April 1948   Flagstad   LP: EMI EX 29 12273/29 10373
                                      LP: Angel 6158
                                      CD: EMI CDH 763 0302

TRADITIONAL

Song of the Volga Boatman

October   Christoff   78: HMV DB 21305
1950   45: HMV 7R 143
                                      45: HMV (France) ESBF 17028
                                      45: HMV (Japan) HJ 1003
                                      LP: EMI RLS 735/1C 147 03336-03337M
                                      CD: EMI CDH 764 2522

Lovro von Matacic
1899-1985
PHILHARMONIA ORCHESTRA

A NEW LP RECORDING
The Great Scenes from "Arabella"

RICHARD STRAUSS

Arabella	ELISABETH SCHWARZKOPF
Mandryka	JOSEF METTERNICH
Matteo	NICOLAI GEDDA
Zdenka	ANNY FELBERMAYER
Count	WALTER BERRY
Dominik	HAROLD PROGLHOF
Elmer	
Die Fiakermilli	MIMI COERTSE
Waldner	FREDERICK GUTHRIE

THE PHILHARMONIA ORCHESTRA
conductor
LOVRO VON MATAČIĆ

DAVID OISTRAKH
VLADIMIR JAMPOLSKIJ
Sonatas for Violin and Pianoforte:
In D minor, Op.9 — *Szymanowski*;
In A major — *Franck*
33CX1201

COLUMBIA
33⅓ R.P.M. LONG PLAYING RECORDS

MILY BALAKIREV (1837-1910)

Islamey, Oriental Fantasy arranged by Liapunov

December　　　　　　　　　　　LP: Columbia 33CX 1280
1954　　　　　　　　　　　　　LP: Columbia (Italy) 33QCX 10187
　　　　　　　　　　　　　　　LP: Angel 35291

Overture on Russian Themes

December　　　　　　　　　　　LP: Columbia 33CX 1420
1954　　　　　　　　　　　　　LP: EMI XLP 30107

Russia, Second Overture on Russian Themes

December　　　　　　　　　　　LP: Columbia 33CX 1280
1954　　　　　　　　　　　　　LP: Columbia (Italy) 33QCX 10187
　　　　　　　　　　　　　　　LP: Angel 35291
　　　　　　　　　　　　　　　LP: EMI XLP 30107
　　　　　　　　　　　　　　　CD: EMI CZS 568 5502

Thamar, Symphonic poem

December　　　　　　　　　　　LP: Columbia 33CX 1280
1954　　　　　　　　　　　　　LP: Columbia (Italy) 33QCX 10187
　　　　　　　　　　　　　　　LP: Angel 35291

ALEXANDER BORODIN (1833-1887)

Prince Igor, Overture

September　　　　　　　　　　LP: Columbia 33CX 1654/SAX 2327
1958　　　　　　　　　　　　　LP: Columbia (France) 33FCX 819/SAXF 227
　　　　　　　　　　　　　　　LP: Columbia (Japan) OS 3028
　　　　　　　　　　　　　　　LP: Angel 35768/RL 3101
　　　　　　　　　　　　　　　LP: EMI XLP 30070/SXLP 30070

132 Matacic

Prince Igor, Dance of the Polovtsian Maidens and Polovtsian Dances

September
1958
LP: Columbia 33CX 1654/SAX 2327
LP: Columbia (France) 33FCX 819/SAXF 227
LP: Columbia (Japan) OS 3028
LP: Angel 35768/RL 3101
LP: EMI XLP 30070/SXLP 30070
CD: EMI CZS 568 5502

Prince Igor, Polovtsian March

September
1958
LP: Columbia 33CX 1654/SAX 2327
LP: Columbia (France) 33FCX 819/SAXF 227
LP: Columbia (Japan) OS 3028
LP: Angel 35768/RL 3101
LP: EMI XLP 30070/SXLP 30070

ANTON BRUCKNER (1824-1896)

Symphony No 4 "Romantic"

October-
December
1954
LP: Columbia 33CX 1274-1275
LP: Angel 3548
CD: Testament SBT 1050

Overture in G minor

January
1956
LP: Angel 3548
CD: Testament SBT 1050

Scherzo in D minor (Symphony No 0)

January
1956
LP: Angel 3548
CD: EMI CZS 568 7392

ALEXANDER GLAZUNOV (1865-1936)

Violin Concerto

December 1954	Rabin	LP: Columbia 33CX 1281 CD: EMI CMS 764 1232

Raymonda, Ballet suite

January 1956	LP: HMV CLP 1843/CSD 1590 CD: EMI CZS 568 7392

FRANZ LEHAR (1870-1948)

Die lustige Witwe

July 1962	Schwarzkopf, Steffek, Gedda, Wächter Philharmonia Chorus	LP: EMI AN 101-102/SAN 101-102/SLS 823/ 1C153 00001-00002/2C153 00001-00002 LP: Angel 3630 CD: EMI CDS 747 1788 Excerpts LP: EMI ALP 2252/ASD 2252 LP: Angel 36340/3754

MODEST MUSSORGSKY (1839-1881)

Night on Bare Mountain

September 1958	LP: Columbia 33CX 1654/SAX 2327 LP: Columbia (France) 33FCX 819/SAXF 227 LP: Columbia (Japan) OS 3028 LP: Angel 35768/RL 3101 LP: EMI XLP 30070/SXLP 30070

134   Matacic

NICOLO PAGANINI (1782-1840)

Violin Concerto No 1

December   Rabin   LP: Columbia 33CX 1281
1954   LP: Columbia (Germany) C 70379/33WC 524
                                    LP: Columbia (Japan) XL 5130
                                    LP: Angel 35259
                                    LP: EMI 1C 037 82112
                                    CD: EMI CDF 300 0212/CMS 764 1232

NIKOLAI RIMSKY-KORSAKOV (1844-1908)

Scheherazade

September   LP: Columbia 33CX 1636
1958   LP: Angel 35767
                                    LP: EMI MFP 2013/SIT 60042
                                    CD: EMI CZS 568 0982/CZS 568 7392

Russian Easter Festival Overture

September   LP: Columbia 33CX 1654/SAλ 2327
1958   LP: Columbia (France) 33FCX 819/SAXF 227
                                    LP: Columbia (Japan) OS 3028
                                    LP: Angel 35768/RL 3101
                                    LP: EMI XLP 30070/SXLP 30070
                                    CD: EMI CZS 568 0982

RICHARD STRAUSS (1864-1949)

Arabella, Extracts

September- October 1954	Schwarzkopf, Felbermayer, Gedda, Berry, Metternich	LP: Columbia 33CX 1226/33CX 1897 LP: Columbia (Germany) C 80619/33WSX 571/ C 90406 LP: Columbia (France) 33FCX 385 LP: Angel 35094 LP: World Records OH 199 LP: EMI RLS 751/1C 037 03297M <u>Excerpts</u> 45: Columbia SEL 1579 LP: EMI RLS 154 6133 CD: EMI CDH 761 0012/CDM 565 5772

PIOTR TCHAIKOVSKY (1840-1893)

Hamlet, Fantasy Overture

January
1956

LP: Columbia 33CX 1420
CD: EMI CHS 764 8552/CZS 568 5502/
    CZS 568 7392

The Storm, Overture

January
1956

LP: Columbia 33CX 1420
LP: HMV CLP 1843/CSD 1590
CD: EMI CHS 764 8552/CZS 568 5502/
    CZS 568 7392

Efrem Kurtz
1900-1995

PHILHARMONIA
ORCHESTRA

NEW
LONG PLAYING RECORDS

WARWICK BRAITHWAITE
and the
ROYAL OPERA HOUSE ORCHESTRA
COVENT GARDEN

"Le Cid"—*Massenet*;
Ballet Music, Act 2; Moorish Rhapsody, Act 3;
"Scènes Alsaciennes"—*Massenet*   PMC1013

ANATOLE FISTOULARI
and the
PHILHARMONIA ORCHESTRA

"Romeo and Juliet"—Fantasy Overture—*Tchaikovsky*;
"Hamlet"—Fantasy Overture—*Tchaikovsky*
PMC1014

WILHELM SCHÜCHTER
and the
PHILHARMONIA ORCHESTRA

Danzas Fantásticas—*Turina*;
Danzas Españolas—*Granados, orch. de Grignon*
PMD1018

PARLOPHONE
33⅓ R.P.M.
LONG PLAYING RECORDS

THE PARLOPHONE COMPANY LIMITED,
RECORD DIVISION, 8-11 GREAT CASTLE STREET, LONDON, W.1

JOHANN SEBASTIAN BACH (1685-1750)

Ach Gott vom Himmel sieh' darein, Chorale Prelude arranged by Kurtz

April 1961   LP: EMI XLP 20058/SXLP 20058

SAMUEL BARBER (1910-1981)

Adagio for strings

April 1961   LP: EMI XLP 20058/SXLP 20058

Souvenirs, Ballet suite

March–   LP: HMV BLP 1080
May 1955

LUDWIG VAN BEETHOVEN (1770-1827)

Turkish March (Die Ruinen von Athen)

July 1959   LP: HMV ALP 1798/ASD 376
                                    LP: Capitol G 7220/SG 7220
                                    CD: EMI CDZ 767 2522

HECTOR BERLIOZ (1803-1869)

La damnation de Faust, Marche hongroise

July 1959
LP: HMV ALP 1798/ASD 376
LP: Capitol G 7220/SG 7220
CD: EMI CDZ 767 2522

Les Troyens, Marche troyenne

July 1959
HMV unpublished

EMANUEL CHABRIER (1841-1894)

Joyeuse marche

July 1959
45: HMV 7ER 5211
LP: HMV ALP 1798/ASD 376
LP: Capitol G 7220/SG 7220
CD: EMI CDZ 767 2522

FREDERIC CHOPIN (1810-1849)

Autumn Leaves, various piano pieces orchestrated as a ballet

June 1955
LP: HMV ALP 1301/ENC 121
Excerpt
45: HMV 7EP 7098

ALEXANDER GLAZUNOV (1865-1936)

Bacchanale (The Seasons)

June 1955   LP: HMV ALP 1301/ENC 121

MIKHAIL GLINKA (1804-1857)

A Life for the Tsar, Ballet music arranged by Rimsky-Korsakov and Glazunov

April 1961   LP: HMV ALP 1962/ASD 513
                                   LP: World Records T 623/ST 623
                                   CD: EMI CZS 767 7292

CHARLES GOUNOD (1818-1893)

Faust, Ballet music

April 1961   LP: HMV ALP 1962/ASD 513
                                   LP: World Records T 623/ST 623

DIMITRI KABALEVSKY (1904-1987)

The Comedians, Ballet suite

April 1961   LP: HMV ALP 1981/ASD 532
                                   LP: EMI HQM 1026
                                   CD: EMI CZS 767 7292

ARAM KHACHATURIAN (1903-1978)

Masquerade, Waltz and Galop

April 1961   LP: HMV ALP 2033/ASD 582
                                   CD: EMI CZS 767 7292

Kurtz

PAUL LINCKE (1866-1946)

Lysistrata, Excerpt (Glow Worm Idyll)

June 1955   45: HMV 7EP 7098
                                   LP: HMV ALP 1301/ENC 121

FELIX MENDELSSOHN-BARTHOLDY (1809-1847)

Violin Concerto

April 1958   Menuhin   LP: HMV ALP 1669/ASD 334
                                   LP: Electrola E 91055/STE 91055/
                                       SME 91055
                                   LP: EMI SLS 5106
                                   CD: EMI CDM 769 0032/CZS 478 3092/
                                       CZS 762 5362/CZS 767 3102

GIACOMO MEYERBEER (1791-1864)

Coronation March (Le prophète)

July 1959   45: HMV 7ER 5211
                                   LP: HMV ALP 1798/ASD 376
                                   LP: Capitol G 7220/SG 7220
                                   CD: EMI CDZ 767 2522

WOLFGANG AMADEUS MOZART (1756-1791)

Andante for flute and orchestra

December 1957	Shaffer	LP: HMV ALP 1676 LP: EMI XLP 30150/SXLP 30150

Flute Concerto No 1

November-December 1957	Shaffer	LP: HMV ALP 1676 LP: EMI XLP 30150/SXLP 30150

Flute Concerto No 2

December 1957	Shaffer	LP: HMV ALP 1676 LP: EMI XLP 30150/SXLP 30150

Piano Concerto No 24

May 1966	A.Fischer	LP: Columbia SAX 5287 CD: EMI CDZ 767 0012

Piano Concerto No 27

May 1966	A.Fischer	LP: Columbia SAX 5287 CD: EMI CDZ 767 0012

SERGEI PROKOFIEV (1891-1953)

Symphony No 1 "Classical"

March 1957
45: HMV 7ER 5175/RES 4275
LP: HMV ALP 1554/ASD 263
LP: World Records T 995/ST 995
LP: EMI XLP 30266/SXLP 30266/CFP 40004
CD: EMI CZS 767 7292

The Love of 3 Oranges, March

July 1959
LP: HMV ALP 1798/ASD 376
LP: Capitol G 7220/SG 7220
CD: EMI CDZ 767 2522

Peter and the Wolf

April 1959   Flanders
LP: HMV ALP 1728/ASD 299
LP: EMI ESD 7114

Romeo and Juliet, Ballet suite

June 1963
LP: HMV CLP 1831/CSD 1585
LP: World Records T 684/ST 684
CD: EMI CDM 764 1882/CDEMX 2194

NIKOLAI RIMSKY-KORSAKOV (1844-1908)

Le coq d'or, Suite

April 1961-
March 1962
LP: HMV ALP 1981/ASD 532
LP: EMI XLP 30076/SXLP 30076
CD: EMI CZS 568 0982/CZS 767 7292

Le coq d'or, Wedding March

July 1959
LP: HMV ALP 1798/ASD 376
LP: Capitol G 7220/SG 7220
CD: EMI CDZ 767 2522

Dubinushka

June-
July 1963
LP: HMV ALP 2033/ASD 582
LP: EMI XLP 30076/SXLP 30076
CD: EMI CZS 568 0982/CZS 767 7292

The Snow Maiden, Suite

June-
July 1963
LP: HMV ALP 2033/ASD 582
LP: EMI CZS 568 0982/CZS 767 7292
Excerpt
LP: EMI XLP 30076/SXLP 30076

Tsar Sultan, Suite

June-
July 1963
LP: HMV ALP 2033/ASD 582
LP: EMI XLP 30076/SXLP 30076

ANTON RUBINSTEIN (1829-1894)

Melody in F, arrangement

June 1955
HMV unpublished

CAMILLE SAINT-SAENS (1835-1921)

Le carnaval des animaux

| April | H.Menuhin, | LP: HMV ALP 1278/ASD 299 |
| 1959 | Simon | LP: EMI ESD 7114 |

The Swan (Le carnaval des animaux)

June 1955
45: HMV 7EP 7098
LP: HMV ALP 1301/ENC 121

FRANZ SCHUBERT (1797-1828)

Marche militaire, arranged by Guiraud

July 1959
LP: HMV ALP 1798/ASD 376
LP: Capitol G 7220/SG 7220
CD: EMI CDZ 767 2522

DIMITRI SHOSTAKOVITCH (1906-1975)

Symphony No 1

March 1957
LP: HMV ALP 1554/ASD 263
LP: World Records T 995/ST 995
LP: EMI CFP 40004
CD: EMI CZS 767 7292

Symphony No 10

March 1955
LP: HMV ALP 1322
LP: EMI HQM 1034

The Age of Gold, Suite

March 1955
LP: HMV BLP 1080
LP: EMI HQM 1026

JOHN PHILIP SOUSA (1854-1932)

Stars and Stripes Forever, March

July 1959
45: HMV 7ER 5211
LP: HMV ALP 1798/ASD 376
LP: Capitol G 7220/SG 7220
CD: EMI CDZ 767 2522

JOHANN STRAUSS I (1804-1849)

Radetzky March

July 1959
45: HMV 7ER 5211
LP: HMV ALP 1798/ASD 376
LP: Capitol G 7220/SG 7220
CD: EMI CDZ 767 2522

IGOR STRAVINSKY (1882-1971)

Petrushka (1947 version)

April 1957
LP: HMV ALP 1503
LP: EMI ENC 111/XLP 30029

2 Suites for small orchestra

December 1957
45: HMV 7ER 5122
LP: EMI HQM 1026

PIOTR TCHAIKOVSKY (1840-1893)

Casse Noisette, selection

March 1958	Chorus	LP: HMV ALP 1609/ASD 289 LP: Capitol G 7149/SG 7149 LP: EMI SLS 859 Excerpts CD: EMI CDZ 762 8612

Marche slave

July 1959	LP: HMV ALP 1798/ASD 376 LP: Capitol G 7220/SG 7220 CD: EMI CDZ 767 2522

Russian Dance, arranged by Schmid

June 1955	45: HMV 7EP 7098 LP: HMV ALP 1301/ENC 121

Sleeping Beauty, selection

April 1959	Menuhin	LP: HMV ALP 1790/ASD 371 LP: EMI SLS 859 Excerpts CD: EMI CDZ 762 8612

Sleeping Beauty, Adagio

June 1955	LP: HMV ALP 1301/ENC 121

Swan Lake, selection

March- April 1958	Menuhin	LP: HMV ALP 1644/ASD 271 LP: EMI SLS 859/CFP 40296 Excerpts CD: EMI CDZ 762 8612

GIUSEPPE VERDI (1813-1901)

Aida, Grand March

July 1959   LP: HMV ALP 1798/ASD 376
                             LP: Capitol G 7220/SG 7220
                             CD: EMI CDZ 767 2522

Otto Ackermann
1909-1960

PHILHARMONIA
ORCHESTRA

*Glorious performances
of your favourite classical works*

OTTO KLEMPERER
conducting the PHILHARMONIA ORCHESTRA
Symphony No. 5 in C minor — *Beethoven* 33C1051
Symphony No. 7 in A — *Beethoven* 33CX1379

HERBERT VON KARAJAN
conducting the PHILHARMONIA ORCHESTRA
Symphony No. 4 in E minor — *Brahms* 33CX1363

IGOR MARKEVITCH
conducting the FRENCH NATIONAL RADIO ORCHESTRA
Symphony No. 8 in B minor ("Unfinished") — *Schubert*
Symphony No. 4 in A ("Italian") — *Mendelssohn* 33CX1394

GEZA ANDA
with the PHILHARMONIA ORCHESTRA
conducted by OTTO ACKERMANN
Concerto No. 1 in E flat — *Liszt*
Hungarian Fantasia — *Liszt* 33CX1363

DAVID OISTRAKH
with the PHILHARMONIA ORCHESTRA
conducted by JEAN MARTINON
Symphonie espagnole — *Lalo* 33CX1246

COLUMBIA
33⅓ r.p.m. Long Playing Records

Columbia Graphophone Company Limited, Record Division, 8-11 Gt. Castle St., London, W.1

JOHANN SEBASTIAN BACH (1685-1750)

Double Violin Concerto

November 1955	Kogan, E.Gilels	LP: Columbia 33CX 1373 LP: Columbia (Germany) C 70427

Violin Concerto in E

November 1955	Kogan	LP: Columbia 33CX 1373 LP: Columbia (Germany) C 70427

EDVARD GRIEG (1843-1907)

Piano Concerto

September 1953	Moiseiwitsch	LP: HMV CLP 1008 LP: Electrola E 80046/WCLP 1008 LP: HMV (France) FELP 126

FRANZ JOSEF HAYDN (1732-1809)

Symphony No 100 "Military"

November 1955	Columbia unpublished

Ackermann

RICHARD HEUBERGER (1850-1914)

Der Opernball, Excerpt (Im chambre séparée)

July 1957	Schwarzkopf	45: Columbia SEL 1648/ESL 6267
		LP: Columbia 33CX 1570/SAX 2283
		LP: Columbia (France) SAXF 158
		LP: Columbia (Austria) SVP 1180
		LP: Angel 35696/3754
		LP: EMI ASD 2807
		CD: EMI CDC 747 2842/CDM 565 5772

FRANZ LEHAR (1870-1948)

Giuditta, Excerpt (Meine Lippen, sie küssen so heiss)

July 1957	Schwarzkopf	45: Columbia SEL 1648/ESL 6267
	Chorus	LP: Columbia 33CX 1570/SAX 2283
		LP: Columbia (France) SAXF 158
		LP: Columbia (Austria) SVP 1180
		LP: Angel 35696
		LP: EMI ASD 2807
		CD: EMI CDC 747 2842

Der Graf von Luxemburg, Excerpts (Heut' noch werd' ich Ehefrau!; Hoch, Evoe, Angele!)

July 1957	Schwarzkopf	45: Columbia SEL 1652/ESL 6270
	Chorus	LP: Columbia 33CX 1570/SAX 2283
		LP: Columbia (France) SAXF 158
		LP: Columbia (Austria) SVP 1180
		LP: Angel 35696
		LP: EMI ASD 2807
		CD: EMI CDC 747 2842

Das Land des Lächelns

April– June 1953	Schwarzkopf, Loose, Gedda, Kunz BBC Chorus	LP: Columbia 33CX 1114-1115 LP: Columbia (Germany) C 80514-80515/ 33WSX 535-536 LP: Columbia (France) 33FCX 288-289 LP: Angel 3507 LP: EMI SXDW 3044 CD: EMI CHS 763 5232 Excerpts 45: Columbia SEL 1556 LP: Columbia 33CX 1712 LP: Columbia (Germany) C 80587/33WSX 563 LP: EMI SLS 5250/RLS 763

Die lustige Witwe

April 1953	Schwarzkopf, Loose, Gedda, Kunz BBC Chorus	LP: Columbia 33CX 1051-1052 LP: Columbia (Germany) C 80516-80517 LP: Columbia (Italy) 33QCX 10050-10051 LP: Columbia (Austria) 33VCX 515-516 LP: Columbia (Japan) XL 5077-5078 LP: Angel 3501 LP: EMI SXDW 3045 CD: EMI CDH 769 5202 Excerpts 78: Columbia LX 1597 45: Columbia SEL 1559/SCB 113/SCD 2083 LP: Columbia 33CX 1712 LP: Columbia (Germany) C 80587/33WSX 563 LP: EMI RLS 763 CD: EMI CDM 763 6572/CMS 763 7902

Der Zarewitsch, Excerpt (Einer wird kommen)

July 1957	Schwarzkopf	45: Columbia SEL 1652/ESL 6270 LP: Columbia 33CX 1570/SAX 2283 LP: Columbia (France) SAXF 158 LP: Columbia (Austria) SVP 1180 LP: Angel 35696 LP: EMI ASD 2807 CD: EMI CDC 747 2842

FRANZ LISZT (1811-1886)

Piano Concerto No 1

May 1955   Anda   LP: Columbia 33CX 1366
                                      LP: Columbia (Italy) 33QCX 10258
                                      LP: Columbia (Japan) ZL 111
                                      LP: Angel 35268
                                      CD: Testament SBT 1071

Hungarian Fantasia

May 1955   Anda   LP: Columbia 33CX 1366
                                      LP: Columbia (Italy) 33QCX 10258
                                      LP: Angel 35268/RL 3048
                                      CD: Testament SBT 1071

ALBERT LORTZING (1801-1851)

Der Waffenschmied, Excerpt (Auch ich war ein Jüngling mit lockigem Haar)

April 1953   Kunz   45: Columbia SEL 1608
                                      LP: Columbia (Germany) C 70407
                                      LP: Columbia (Austria) VS 811
                                      LP: EMI 1C 147 03580-03581M
                                      CD: Testament SBT 1059

Der Wildschütz, Excerpt (Fünftausend Thaler!)

April 1953   Kunz   78: Columbia LB 143
                                      LP: Columbia (Germany) C 70407
                                      LP: Columbia (Austria) VS 811
                                      LP: EMI 1C 147 03580-03581M
                                      LP: Preiser LV 18
                                      CD: Testament SBT 1059

Zar und Zimmermann, Excerpt (O sancta justitia!)

April 1953   Kunz   45: Columbia SEL 1608
                             LP: Columbia (Germany) C 70407
                             LP: Columbia (Austria) VS 811
                             LP: EMI 147 03580-03581M
                             CD: Testament SBT 1059

CARL MILLOECKER (1842-1899)

Die Dubarry, Excerpt (Ich schenk' mein Herz)

July 1957   Schwarzkopf   LP: Columbia 33CX 1570/ASD 2283
                             LP: Columbia (France) SAXF 158
                             LP: Columbia (Austria) SVP 1180
                             LP: Angel 35696/3754
                             LP: EMI ASD 2807
                             CD: EMI CDC 747 2842

Die Dubarry, Excerpt (Was ich im Leben beginne)

July 1957   Schwarzkopf   LP: Columbia 33CX 1570/SAX 2283
              Chorus   LP: Columbia (France) SAXF 158
                             LP: Columbia (Austria) SVP 1180
                             LP: Angel 35696/3754
                             LP: EMI ASD 2807
                             CD: EMI CDC 747 2842

WOLFGANG AMADEUS MOZART (1756-1791)

Piano Concerto No 15

September 1953	Solomon	LP: HMV ALP 1194 LP: Victor LHMV 12 LP: HMV (Italy) QALP 10167 LP: International Angel AHA 3 LP: EMI RLS 726/1C 147 50183-50184M CD: EMI CDH 763 7072

Violin Concerto No 3

November 1955	Kogan	LP: Columbia 33CX 1395 LP: Columbia (Germany) C 70378

Ch'io mi scordi di te?, Concert aria

May 1955	Schwarzkopf, Anda	Columbia unpublished

JACQUES OFFENBACH (1819-1880)

Orfée aux enfers, Overture

July 1959	Columbia unpublished

SERGEI RACHMANINOV (1873-1943)

Piano Concerto No 2

November 1955	Malinin	LP: Columbia 33CX 1369

MAURICE RAVEL (1875-1937)

Tzigane for violin and orchestra

November 1955	Kogan	Columbia unpublished

ROBERT SCHUMANN (1810-1856)

Piano Concerto

September 1953   Moiseiwitsch   LP: HMV CLP 1008
　　　　　　　　　　　　　　　　　　LP: Victor LBC 1081
　　　　　　　　　　　　　　　　　　LP: Electrola E 80046/WCLP 1008

RUDOLF SIECZYNSKI (1879-1952)

Wien, du Stadt meiner Träume

July 1957   Schwarzkopf   45: Columbia SEL 1648/ESL 6267/SCD 2128
　　　　　　　Chorus　　　　　LP: Columbia 33CX 1570/SAX 2283
　　　　　　　　　　　　　　　　LP: Columbia (France) SAXF 158
　　　　　　　　　　　　　　　　LP: Columbia (Austria) SVP 1180
　　　　　　　　　　　　　　　　LP: Angel 35696
　　　　　　　　　　　　　　　　LP: EMI ASD 2807
　　　　　　　　　　　　　　　　CD: EMI CDC 747 2842

BEDRICH SMETANA (1824-1884)

The Moldau (Ma Vlast)

September 1953   45: Columbia SEL 1619
　　　　　　　　　　45: Columbia (Italy) SEBQ 199
　　　　　　　　　　LP: Columbia 33C 1042
　　　　　　　　　　LP: Columbia (Italy) 33QC 5042

From Bohemia's Woods and Fields (Ma Vlast)

September 1954   LP: Columbia 33C 1042
　　　　　　　　　　LP: Columbia (Italy) 33QC 5042

160 Ackermann

JOHANN STRAUSS II (1825-1899)

Casanova, Excerpt (Laura's Song and Nuns' Chorus)

July 1957	Schwarzkopf Chorus	45: Columbia SEL 1642/ESL 6263/SCD 2128 LP: Columbia 33CX 1570/SAX 2283 LP: Columbia (France) SAXF 158 LP: Columbia (Austria) SVP 1180 LP: Angel 35696 LP: EMI ASD 2807/YKM 5014 CD: EMI CDC 747 2842/CDCFP 4499

Die Fledermaus

June-
July 1959
	Lipp, Scheyrer,
	C.Ludwig, Dermota,
	Terkal, Kunz,
	Berry
	Philharmonia
	Chorus
		LP: Columbia 33CX 1688-1689/
		  SAX 2336-2337
		LP: Columbia (Germany) C 80596-80597/
		  STC 80596-80597/SCXW 7606-7607
		LP: EMI 1C 147 01652-01653/CFPD 4702
		CD: EMI CDCFPD 4702
		Excerpts
		LP: EMI XLP 20091/SXLP 20091

Eine Nacht in Venedig

May- September 1954	Schwarzkopf, Loose, Gedda, Kunz, Dönch Chorus	LP: Columbia 33CX 1224-1225 LP: Columbia (Germany) C 80510-80511/ 33WSX 531-532 LP: EMI SXDW 3043 LP: Angel 3530 CD: EMI CDH 769 5302 Excerpts LP: EMI SMVP 6075/RLS 763

Eine Nacht in Venedig, Excerpt (Seht, o seht!)

July 1957	Schwarzkopf	Columbia unpublished

Wiener Blut

May 1954   Schwarzkopf, Köth, Loose, Gedda, Kunz, Dönch, Chorus

- LP: Columbia 33CX 1186-1187
- LP: Columbia (Germany) C 80518-80519/ 33WSX 539-540
- LP: Angel 3519
- LP: EMI SXDW 3042
- CD: EMI CDH 769 5292

Excerpts
- LP: Columbia (Germany) 33WSX 608
- LP: EMI SMVP 6075/1C 047 01954/RLS 763/ 1C 147 03580-03581M/RLS 154 6133

Der Zigeunerbaron

May-September 1954   Schwarzkopf, Köth, Sinclair, Gedda, Kunz, Prey, Chorus

- LP: Columbia 33CX 1329-1330
- LP: Columbia (Germany) C 80520-80521/ 33WSX 541-542
- LP: Columbia (Japan) XL 5127-5128
- LP: Angel 3566
- LP: EMI SXDW 3046
- CD: EMI CHS 769 5262

Excerpts
- LP: EMI SLS 5250/RLS 763

Der Zigeunerbaron, Excerpt (So elend und treu)

July 1957	Schwarzkopf	Columbia unpublished

RICHARD STRAUSS (1864-1949)

4 letzte Lieder

September 1953	Schwarzkopf	LP: Columbia 33CX 1107 LP: Columbia (Germany) 33WCX 1107 LP: Columbia (France) 33FCX 294 LP: Angel 35084/38266 LP: EMI RLS 751/100 8651/ 2C 061 01208 CD: EMI CDH 761 0012 CD: NotaBlu 935.0932

Capriccio, Excerpt (Morgen mittag um elf?)

September 1953	Schwarzkopf	LP: Columbia 33CX 1107 LP: Columbia (Germany) 33WCX 1107 LP: Columbia (France) 33FCX 294 LP: Angel 35084/38266 LP: EMI RLS 751/100 8651/2C061 01208 CD: EMI CDH 761 0012 CD: NotaBlu 935.0932

FRANZ VON SUPPE (1819-1895)

Boccaccio, Excerpt (Hab' ich nur deine Liebe)

July 1957	Schwarzkopf	45: Columbia SEL 1652/ESL 6270 LP: Columbia 33CX 1570/SAX 2283 LP: Columbia (France) SAXF 158 LP: Columbia (Austria) SVP 1180 LP: Angel 35696 LP: EMI ASD 2807 CD: EMI CDC 747 2842

PIOTR TCHAIKOVSKY (1840-1893)

Sérénade mélancolique for violin and orchestra

November 1955	Kogan	Columbia unpublished

RICHARD WAGNER (1813-1883)

Der fliegende Holländer, Excerpt (Mögst du, mein Kind?)

July 1957	Edelmann	LP: Columbia 33CX 1568
		LP: Angel 35571

Lohengrin, Excerpts (Gott grüss' euch, liebe Männer!; Mein Herr und Gott!)

July 1957	Edelmann	LP: Columbia 33CX 1568
		LP: Angel 35571

Parsifal, Excerpt (Das ist Karfreitagszauber, Herr!)

July 1957	Edelmann	LP: Columbia 33CX 1568
		LP: Angel 35571

Tannhäuser, Excerpt (Gar viel und schön)

July 1957	Edelmann	LP: Columbia 33CX 1568
		LP: Angel 35571

Die Walküre, Excerpt (Leb wohl, du kühnes herrliches Kind)

July 1957	Edelmann	LP: Columbia 33CX 1568
		LP: Angel 35571

164 Ackermann

CARL ZELLER (1842-1898)

Der Obersteiger, Excerpt (Sei nicht bös'!)

July 1957   Schwarzkopf   45: Columbia SEL 1648/ESL 6267
                                    LP: Columbia 33CX 1570/SAX 2283
                                    LP: Columbia (France) SAXF 158
                                    LP: Columbia (Austria) SVP 1180
                                    LP: Angel 35696/3754
                                    LP: EMI ASD 2807/CFP 4277/SEOM 1
                                    CD: EMI CDC 747 2842/CDCFP 4277

Der Vogelhändler, Excerpt (Ich bin die Christel von der Post)

July 1957   Schwarzkopf   45: Columbia SEL 1642/ESL 6263
                                    LP: Columbia (France) SAXF 158
                                    LP: Columbia (Austria) SVP 1180
                                    LP: Angel 35696/3754
                                    LP: EMI ASD 2807
                                    CD: EMI CDC 747 2842

Der Vogelhändler, Excerpt (Schenkt man sich Rosen im Tirol)

July 1957   Schwarzkopf   45: Columbia SEL 1642/ESL 6263
                                    LP: Columbia 33CX 1570/SAX 2283
                                    LP: Columbia (France) SAXF 158
                                    LP: Columbia (Austria) SVP 1180
                                    LP: Angel 35696
                                    LP: EMI ASD 2807
                                    CD: EMI CDC 747 2842

'DER ZIGEUNERBARON'

Johann Strauss

ELISABETH SCHWARZKOPF........SAFFI
NICOLAI GEDDA.......SÁNDOR BARINKAY
ERICH KUNZ..........KÁLMÁN ZSUPÁN
ERIKA KÖTH...................ARSENA

PHILHARMONIA ORCHESTRA and CHORUS
conducted by OTTO ACKERMANN
33CX1329-30

YOU MAY BE PLANNING TO BUY STEREO EQUIPMENT.
REMEMBER THAT MOST ORDINARY LPs AND EPs SOUND
EVEN BETTER ON GOOD STEREOPHONIC REPRODUCERS.

Anatole Fistoulari
1907-1995

PHILHARMONIA
ORCHESTRA

NATHAN MILSTEIN

VIOLIN CONCERTOS
Philharmonia Orchestra/Anatole Fistoulari
BRAHMS: Concerto in D major   SP8560 (stereo) or P8560 (mono)

Philharmonia Orchestra/Leon Barzin
MENDELSSOHN: Concerto in E minor;
BRUCH: Concerto No. 1 in G minor   SP8518 (stereo) or P8518 (mono)

Pittsburgh Symphony Orchestra/William Steinberg
BEETHOVEN: Concerto in D   P8313 (mono only)

DVŎŘÁK: Concerto in A minor;
GLAZOUNOV: Concerto in A minor   SP8382 (stereo) or P8382 (mono)

TCHAIKOVSKY: Concerto in D   SP8512 (stereo) or P8512 (mono)

with LEON POMMERS

VIOLIN AND PIANO SONATAS
TARTINI: The Devil's Trill; *VIVALDI:* A major;
CORELLI: La Follia; *GEMINIANI:* A major   SP8481 (stereo) or P8481 (mono)

ENCORES
KREISLER: Praeludium and Allegro; Siciliano and Rigaudon;
SCHUMANN: Abendlied; *SZYMANOWSKI:* Nocturne and Tarantella;
HANDEL: Larghetto; *LECLAIR:* Tambourin; *MENDELSSOHN:* Song without words;
BRAHMS: Waltz, No. 15 in A flat (trs. A major); *POLDINI:* Poupée valsante
SP8536 (stereo) or P8536 (mono)

E.M.I. RECORDS LTD., E.M.I. HOUSE, 20 MANCHESTER SQUARE, LONDON, W.1

VINCENZO BELLINI (1801-1835)

I Capuleti ed i Montecchi, Excerpt (Ah quante volte!)

May 1951	Carosio	78: HMV DB 21336
		LP: HMV (Italy) QALP 5342/QUAL 5342
		LP: EMI 3C 053 00734/EX 769 7411
		CD: EMI CHS 769 7412

La sonnambula, Excerpt (Ah non credea mirarti!)

October 1950	Del Pozo	78: HMV C 4237
		45: HMV 7P 146

ALEXANDER BORODIN (1833-1887)

Nocturne (String Quartet in D), arranged by Tcherepnin

July 1956- March 1957	LP: HMV ALP 1582 LP: EMI XLP 30119/SXLP 30119

Prince Igor, Excerpts (I hate a dreary life; No sleep, no rest!)

December 1958	Ladysz	LP: Columbia 33CX 1678

170   Fistoulari

JOHANNES BRAHMS (1833-1897)

Piano Concerto No 2

August 1977	Vered	LP: Decca PFS 4428

Violin Concerto

June 1960	Milstein	LP: Capitol P 8560/SP 8560
		LP: EMI 18 00191
		CD: EMI CDM 253 6572/ZDMF 764 8302

MAX BRUCH (1838-1920)

Violin Concerto No 1

March 1977	Wanawi	RCA Japan

ERNEST CHAUSSON (1855-1899)

Poème for violin and orchestra

June 1963	Milstein	LP: Angel 36005/32056
		LP: EMI XLP 30159/SXLP 30159

ERNO DOHNANYI (1877-1960)

Variations on a Nursery Song

September 1952	Jacquinot	LP: Parlophone PMC 1005

GAETONO DONIZETTI (1797-1848)

Don Pasquale, Excerpt (Quel guardo il cavaliere!)

October 1950	Del Pozo	78: HMV C 4237 45: HMV 7P 146

ALEXANDER GLAZUNOV (1865-1935)

Stenka Razin, Symphonic poem

March 1956- March 1957	LP: HMV ALP 1582 LP: EMI XLP 30119/SXLP 30119

Valse de concert No 1

March 1957	45: HMV 7EB 6028/RES 4255 LP: EMI XLP 30119/SXLP 30119

CHRISTOPH WILLIBALD GLUCK (1714-1787)

Alceste, Excerpt (Divinités du Styx!)

December 1952	Flagstad	HMV unpublished

Iphigenia in Aulis, Excerpt (O Diana, dea spietate!)

March 1951	Christoff	LP: EMI RLS 735 CD: EMI CDH 565 5002

Fistoulari

CHARLES GOUNOD (1818-1893)

Faust, Excerpt (Le veau d'or)

| August 1952 | Rossi-Lemeni Chorus | 78: HMV DA 2050
LP: HMV ALP 1074
LP: EMI 3C 053 03249 |

ENRIQUE GRANADOS (1867-1916)

La maja y el ruisenor (Goyescas)

| March 1950 | De los Angeles | 78: HMV DB 21069
CD: EMI CDH 764 0282 |

EDVARD GRIEG (1843-1907)

Hearts' Wounds (Elegiac Melodies)

March- July 1953	LP: HMV ALP 1570

Last Spring (Elegiac Melodies)

July 1956	LP: HMV ALP 1570

Holberg Suite

December 1952- December 1954	45: HMV 7ER 5172 LP: HMV ALP 1570
June- July 1963	LP: EMI XLP 20058/SXLP 20058

4 Norwegian Dances, arranged by Sitt

February 1952	LP: Parlophone PMD 1025

Peer Gynt, Suite No 1

February 1952	LP: Parlophone PMD 1025

Symphonic Dance No 4

March 1957	LP: HMV ALP 1570

Fistoulari

GEORGE FRIDERIC HANDEL (1685-1759)

Messiah, Excerpt (I know that my redeemer liveth)

December   Flagstad   CD: Testament SBT 1018
1952

ARTHUR HONEGGER (1892-1955)

Concertino for piano and orchestra

October   Jacquinot   LP: MGM E 3041
1951

FRANZ LISZT (1811-1886)

Piano Concerto No 1

April   Cherkassky   78: HMV DB 9763-9764
1952   LP: HMV BLP 1013
                                 LP: Electrola E 70024
                                 CD: Testament SBT 1033

Les Préludes

November   LP: Parlophone PMD 1019
1952

Mazeppa

November   LP: Parlophone PMD 1019
1952

Totentanz for piano and orchestra

September   Jacquinot   LP: Parlophone PMD 1026
1952

JULES MASSENET (1842-1912)

Manon, Excerpt (Adieu notre petite table)

| May 1951 | Carosio
<u>Sung in Italian</u> | 78: HMV DB 21336
LP: EMI 3C 053 00734 |

FELIX MENDELSSOHN-BARTHOLDY (1809-1847)

Violin Concerto

| June 1978 | Wanawi | RCA Japan |

GIACOMO MEYERBEER (1791-1864)

Robert le diable, Excerpt (Nonnes qui reposez)

| December 1958 | Ladysz | Columbia unpublished |

DARIUS MILHAUD (1892-1974)

Piano Concerto No 1

| October 1951 | Jacquinot | LP: MGM E 3041 |

OTTO NICOLAI (1810-1849)

Die lustigen Weiber von Windsor, Overture

| August 1951 | | LP: Parlophone PMC 1031 |

Fistoulari

NICOLO PAGANINI (1782-1840)

Violin Concerto No 2

October 1950	Menuhin	78: HMV DB 9588-9591 45: Victor WHMV 1015 LP: HMV BLP 1018 LP: Victor LHMV 1015 LP: Electrola E 70026 LP: HMV (France) FBLP 1006 LP: Toshiba EAC 60230-60239 <u>Third movement</u> 78: HMV DB 20406

SERGEI PROKOFIEV (1891-1953)

Lieutenant Kijé, Excerpts (Kijé's Wedding; Troika; Kijé's Burial)

April 1959   45: HMV 7ER 5145
                   LP: EMI XLP 30119/SXLP 30119

EMIL REZNICEK (1860-1945)

Donna Diana, Overture

August 1951   LP: Parlophone PMC 1031

NIKOLAI RIMSKY-KORSAKOV (1844-1908)

Baba Yaga

November 1952   LP: Parlophone PMD 1028

May Night, Overture

August 1951   LP: Parlophone PMC 1031
                               LP: EMI XLP 30031

Piano Concerto

September 1952   Jacquinot   LP: Parlophone PMD 1026

Skaska (Fairy Tale)

November 1952   LP: Parlophone PMD 1028
                               LP: EMI XLP 30031

The Snow Maiden, Suite

November 1952   LP: Parlophone PMD 1028

CAMILLE SAINT-SAENS (1835-1921)

Violin Concerto No 3

June 1963   Milstein   LP: Angel 36005/32056
                               LP: EMI XLP 30159/SXLP 30159
                               CD: EMI ZDMF 764 8302

178   Fistoulari

RICHARD STRAUSS (1864-1949)

Burleske for piano and orchestra

September   Jacquinot   LP: Parlophone PMC 1005
1952

PIOTR TCHAIKOVSKY (1840-1893)

Violin Concerto

March 1977   Wanawi   LP: Trio PA 1149

Andante cantabile (String Quartet in D), arranged by Schmid

July 1963   LP: EMI XLP 20058/SXLP 20058

Evgeny Onegin, Excerpt (Everyone knows love on earth)

December   Ladysz   LP: Columbia 33CX 1678
1958

Hamlet, Fantasy Overture

July 1952   LP: Parlophone PMC 1014

Iolantha, Excerpt (What is in store?)

December   Ladysz   LP: Columbia 33CX 1678
1958

Romeo and Juliet, Fantasy Overture

July 1952   LP: Parlophone PMC 1014

The Slippers, Suite

January
1953

LP: Parlophone PMC 1028

The Storm, Overture

February
1956

LP: HMV ALP 1582
LP: EMI XLP 30101/SXLP 30101

Suite No 4 "Mozartiana"

January
1953

LP: Parlophone PMC 1028
LP: EMI XLP 30031

Swan Lake, Waltz

March 1957

45: HMV 7EB 6028/RES 4255
LP: EMI XLP 30119/SXLP 30119

GIUSEPPE VERDI (1813-1901)

Ave Maria, Song

May 1951   Carosio   45: HMV 7ER 5162

Don Carlo, Excerpt (Ella giammai m'amò)

December   Ladysz   LP: Columbia 33CX 1678
1958

Ernani, Excerpt (L'offeso ognor, signori!)

March 1951   Christoff   78: HMV DB 21424
                                  45: HMV (France) 7RF 264
                                  45: HMV (Italy) 7RF 264
                                  LP: EMI RLS 735/1C 147 03336-03337M
                                  CD: EMI CDH 565 5002

180   Fistoulari

La forza del destino, Excerpt (Il santo nome di Dio!)

| August
1952 | Hammond,
Rossi-Lemeni
Covent Garden
Chorus | 78: HMV DB 9779-9780
LP: HMV ALP 1099
LP: HMV (France) FALP 305
LP: HMV (Italy) QALP 10028
LP: EMI 3C 053 01738 |

Nabucco, Excerpt (D'Egitto là sui lidi)

| August
1952 | Rossi-Lemeni
Covent Garden
Chorus | LP: HMV ALP 1099
LP: HMV (France) FALP 305
LP: HMV (Italy) QALP 10033
LP: EMI 3C 053 01738 |

Nabucco, Excerpt (Vieni, o levità!)

| December
1958 | Ladysz | LP: Columbia 33CX 1678 |

Nabucco, Excerpt (Del futuro nel buio discerno)

| August
1952 | Rossi-Lemeni
Covent Garden
Chorus | 78: HMV DB 21610
45: HMV 7R 177
LP: HMV ALP 1099
LP: HMV (France) FALP 305
LP: HMV (Italy) QALP 10028
LP: EMI 3C 053 01738 |

Nabucco, Excerpt (Come notte a sol fulgente)

| August
1952 | Rossi-Lemeni
Covent Garden
Chorus | 78: HMV DB 21610
45: HMV 7R 177
LP: HMV ALP 1099
LP: HMV (France) FALP 305
LP: HMV (Italy) QALP 10028
LP: EMI 3C 053 01738 |

Simone Boccanegra, Excerpt (Il lacerato spirito)

December   Ladysz   LP: Columbia 33CX 1678
1958

La traviata, Excerpt (Ah fors' è lui/Sempre libera!)

May 1951   Carosio   78: HMV DB 21306
                                 45: HMV 7ER 5162

I vespri siciliani, Excerpt (O tu Palermo!)

December   Ladysz   LP: Columbia 33CX 1678
1958

HENRI VIEUXTEMPS (1820-1881)

Violin Concerto No 5

December   Menuhin   LP: HMV ALP 1241
1954

RICHARD WAGNER (1813-1883)

Lohengrin, Excerpt (Einsam in trüben Tagen)

March 1950   De los Angeles   78: HMV DB 21095
                                 LP: EMI 1C 187 30183-30184/29 05583

Tannhäuser, Excerpt (Dich teure Halle!)

March 1950   De los Angeles   78: HMV DB 21095
                                 LP: EMI 1C 187 30183-30184/29 05583

Fistoulari

ERMANNO WOLF-FERRARI (1876-1948)

I gioielli della madonna, Intermezzo

December 1952	HMV unpublished

Il segreto di Susanna, Overture

August 1951	LP: Parlophone PMC 1031

MISCELLANEOUS

Ah sweet mystery of life!

September 1950	Peerce	78: HMV DA 2010 LP: Victor LM 2101 LP: EMI EX 769 7411 CD: EMI CHS 769 7412

Amapola

September 1950	Peerce	HMV unpublished

La danza

September 1950	Peerce	LP: Victor LM 2101

Mattinata

September 1950	Peerce	LP: Victor LM 2101

O sole mio

September   Peerce   LP: Victor LM 2101
1950

Serenade

September   Peerce   HMV unpublished
1950

Silver threads among the gold

September   Peerce   LP: RCA VIC 1553
1950

Song of songs

September   Peerce   78: HMV DA 2010
1950   LP: Victor LM 2101
                               LP: RCA VIC 1553
                               LP: EMI SLS 50261

Sylvia

September   Peerce   HMV unpublished
1950

Torna a Surriento

September   Peerce   78: HMV DA 1962
1950   LP: Victor LM 2101

Valencia

September   Peerce   LP: Victor LM 2101
1950

When you and I were young

September   Peerce   LP: RCA VIC 1553
1950

George Weldon
1908-1963
PHILHARMONIA ORCHESTRA

✴✴✴ and now COLUMBIA 7 inch Extended Play Records

✯ ✯ ✯ ✯ ✯

Now, as a result of the latest recording advances made by Columbia technicians, it has been possible to record on a single 7″ 45 r.p.m. record up to 15 minutes of virtually uninterrupted music.

This newest development means that connoisseurs of classical music and devotees of opera can now obtain, for example, Berlioz' "Béatrice et Bénédict" and other full-length overtures, or two operatic arias *on one side* of a 7″ 45 r.p.m. record. Similarly, extended play records give collectors of light music, popular tunes and jazz classics—4 on each record.

All this in addition to superb quality reproduction, silent surfaces, flexibility plus lightness and compactness, make these new Columbia Extended Play records a splendid addition to every collection.

7-inch LIGHT BLUE LABEL 12/- (plus 3/11d. tax)
7-inch BLACK LABEL ... 8/- (plus 2/7½d. tax)
7-inch DARK BLUE LABEL 8/6 (plus 2/9½d. tax)
7-inch GREEN LABEL ... 7/- (plus 2/3½d. tax)

up to 15 minutes playing time on a single seven-inch 45 R.P.M. record

---

7-INCH LIGHT BLUE LABEL
PAUL KLETZKI
and the PHILHARMONIA ORCHESTRA
Overture "Béatrice et Bénédict"—*Berlioz*;
Ballet Music No. 2 in G major (from "Rosamunde")—*Schubert* - - - - SEL1502

HERBERT VON KARAJAN
and the VIENNA PHILHARMONIC ORCHESTRA
Vienna Blood—Waltz—*J. Strauss, Jr.*
Artist's Life—Waltz—*J. Strauss;*   SEL1503

SIR WILLIAM WALTON
and the PHILHARMONIA ORCHESTRA
Sheep may safely graze (from "The Wise Virgins"—Ballet Suite)—*J. S. Bach arr. Walton*;
Crown Imperial—Coronation March 1937—
Walton - - - - - - SEL1504

7-INCH BLACK LABEL
LUIGI INFANTINO
Santa Lucia—*Cottrau*; Milena—*Infantino*
Marechiare—*Tosti*; Passione—*Bovio*; SEB3502

7-INCH DARK BLUE LABEL
ALCEO GALLIERA
and the PHILHARMONIA ORCHESTRA
Rossini Overtures: "L'Italiana in Algeri";
"La Scala di Seta" - - - - SED5502

WILHELM SCHUECHTER
and the PHILHARMONIA ORCHESTRA
Dances of the Persian Slaves—*Moussorgsky*,
orch. *Rimsky-Korsakov*;
"Coriolan"—Overture—*Beethoven* - SED5503

CONSTANT LAMBERT
and the PHILHARMONIA ORCHESTRA
Morning, Noon and Night in Vienna—
Overture—*von Suppé*;
"Sur la Plage"—Waltz—*Waldteufel*
SED5504

ANDRE KOSTELANETZ
and his Orchestra
The Bee—*Schubert*;
The Flight of the Bumble Bee—*Rimsky-Korsakov*;
Bacchanale (from "Samson et Dalilah")—
Saint-Saëns;
Dance for Six (from "William Tell")—*Rossini*;
Dance of the Sylphs (from "Damnation of Faust")—*Berlioz* - - - - - SED5511

7-INCH GREEN LABEL
EDDIE CALVERT
his Trumpet and his Orchestra
Song of the Golden Trumpet;
Summertime; Some Enchanted Evening;
Mambo in F - - - - - - SEG7501

KEN GRIFFIN
Louise; Side by side; In an 18th Century Drawing Room; Cecile Waltz - - SEG7502

DUKE ELLINGTON
and his Orchestra
The Hawk talks; Fancy Dan; V.I.P.'s Boogie;
Jam with Sam - - - - - SEG7503

FREDDY GARDNER
I'm in the mood for love; Body and Soul;
I only have eyes for you; Valse Vanité
SEG7504

FRANKIE LAINE
Jezebel; High Noon; The Gandy Dancers' Ball;
Jealousy - - - - - - - SEG7505

DORIS DAY
Canadian Capers; You go to my head;
Just one of those things; Crazy Rhythm
SEG7507

QUEEN'S HALL LIGHT ORCHESTRA
conducted by SIDNEY TORCH
Jamaican Rumba; The Boulevardier;
Shooting Star; Dance of an ostracised imp
SEG7508

COLUMBIA 45 R.P.M. ♪ EXTENDED PLAY RECORDS

COLUMBIA GRAPHOPHONE COMPANY LIMITED. RECORD DIVISION, 8-11, GREAT CASTLE STREET, LONDON, W 1

MALCOLM ARNOLD (Born 1921)

Scottish Dance No 1

October   LP: HMV CLP 1645/CSD 1495
1962   LP: World Records T 927/ST 927

JOHANN SEBASTIAN BACH (1685-1750)

Air (Suite No 3)

May 1961   LP: Columbia 33SX 1394/33SX 1436/SCX 3446

Jauchzet Gott in allen Landen, from Cantata No 51

June 1946   Columbia unpublished

Schafe können sicher weiden (The Wise Virgins, arranged by Walton)

July 1951   78: Columbia DB 3164
                                               45: Columbia SED 5509
                                               LP: Columbia 33SX 1032

HECTOR BERLIOZ (1803-1869)

Marche hongroise (La damnation de Faust)

November   78: Columbia DX 1818
1951   78: Columbia (Germany) DWX 5078
                                               LP: Columbia (USA) RL 3042

Weldon

LUIGI BOCCHERINI (1743-1805)

Minuetto (Quintet in E), arrangement

March 1950   78: Columbia DX 1670
                                    45: Columbia SED 5507

JOHANNES BRAHMS (1833-1897)

Hungarian Dance No 3

May 1961   Columbia unpublished

JEREMIAH CLARKE (1659-1707)

Trumpet Voluntary

December   Mortimer   Columbia unpublished
1947

ERIC COATES (1886-1957)

Covent Garden (London Suite); Oxford Street (London Again)

October   LP: HMV CLP 1645/CSD 1495
1962   LP: World Records T 927/ST 927

SAMUEL COLERIDGE-TAYLOR (1875-1912)

Petite Suite de concert

October   45: HMV 7EP 7133/PES 5285
1962   LP: EMI XLP 30123/SXLP 30123/ESD 7161/
                                        CFP 4510

WALFORD DAVIES (1869-1941)

Solemn Melody

March 1950

78: Columbia DX 1681
45: Columbia SED 5507/SCD 2086

LEO DELIBES (1836-1891)

Pizzicato (Sylvia)

March 1956

45: Columbia SED 5547

FREDERICK DELIUS (1862-1934)

La Calinda (Koanga)

May 1961

LP: Columbia 33SX 1436/SCX 3446
LP: EMI XLP 30123/SXLP 30123/CFP 4510
CD: EMI CDEMX 2198

ANTONIN DVORAK (1841-1904)

Carnival Overture

April 1963

LP: Columbia 33SX 1570/SCX 3499

Weldon

EDWARD ELGAR (1857-1934)

Enigma Variations

June- October 1953	LP: Columbia 33SX 1024 LP: EMI MFP 2093 <u>Excerpts</u> 45: Columbia SED 5520/SCD 2139

Sea Pictures

May 1946	Ripley	78: HMV C 3498-3500/C 7638-7640 <u>Where corals lie</u> LP: EMI EX 769 7411 CD: EMI CHS 769 7412

Pomp and Circumstance, March No 1

October 1953	45: Columbia SED 5520 LP: Columbia 33SX 1024 LP: EMI MFP 2093

Pomp and Circumstance, March No 4

November 1953	LP: Columbia 33SX 1024 LP: EMI MFP 2093

Cockaigne Overture

October 1953	LP: Columbia 33SX 1024 LP: EMI MFP 2093

MANUEL DE FALLA (1876-1946)

Ritual Fire Dance (El amor brujo)

May 1961   LP: Columbia 33SX 1436/SCX 3446

CESAR FRANCK (1822-1890)

Variations symphoniques for piano and orchestra

October   Casadesus   78: Columbia LX 8800-8801
1949   78: Columbia (USA) MX 338
                                  LP: Columbia 33CX 1118
                                  LP: Columbia (USA) ML 4298

MIKHAIL GLINKA (1804-1857)

Russlan and Ludmila, Overture

May 1961   LP: Columbia 33SX 1436/SCX 3446

PERCY GRAINGER (1882-1961)

Londonderry Air

March 1956   45: Columbia SED 5547

October   45: HMV 7P 394
1962   LP: HMV CLP 1645/CSD 1495
                                  LP: World Records T 927/ST 927

Mock Morris

May 1961   LP: Columbia 33SX 1436/SCX 3446
                                  LP: EMI XLP 30123/SXLP 30123/CFP 4510

Weldon

ENRIQUE GRANADOS (1867-1916)

Goyescas, Intermezzo

July 1951   78: Columbia DX 1801
                                        78: Columbia (Germany) DWX 5075

EDVARD GRIEG (1843-1907)

2 Elegiac Melodies

May 1961   LP: Columbia 33SX 1378/SCX 3416
                                        LP: EMI CFP 40225

Holberg Suite

May 1961   LP: Columbia 33SX 1378/SCX 3416
                                        LP: EMI CFP 40225

2 Norwegian Melodies

May 1961   LP: Columbia 33SX 1378/SCX 3416
                                        LP: EMI CFP 40225

Sigurd Jorsalfar, Suite

May 1961   LP: Columbia 33SX 1378/SCX 3416
                                        LP: EMI CFP 40225

GEORGE FRIDERIC HANDEL (1685-1759)

Berenice, Minuet

March 1950   78: Columbia DX 1670
                                    45: Columbia SED 5507

Giulio Cesare, Excerpt (Alma del gran Pompeo)

May 1953   Deller   78: HMV C 4222
                                    LP: EMI HLM 7234

Giulio Cesare, Excerpt (Dall' ondoso periglio)

November   Hotter   78: Columbia LX 1538
1951   LP: EMI 1C 147 01633-01634M

Joshua, Excerpt (Shall I in Mamre's fertile plains)

November   Hotter   78: Columbia LX 1516
1951   <u>Sung in German</u>   78: Columbia (Australia) LOX 833
                                    LP: EMI 1C 147 01633-01634M

Messiah, Excerpt (O thou that tellest)

January   Deller   78: HMV C 4222
1953   LP: EMI HLM 7234

Messiah, Excerpt (He was despised)

January   Deller   78: HMV B 10682
1953   LP: EMI HLM 7234

Orlando, Excerpt (Mad Scene)

May 1953   Deller   HMV unpublished

194　Weldon

Samson, Overture

October 1949　　　　　　　　　　　78: Columbia DX 1731

Samson, Excerpt (How willing my paternal love)

November 1951　　Hotter　　　　　78: Columbia LX 1516
　　　　　　　　　Sung in German　78: Columbia (Australia) LOX 833
　　　　　　　　　　　　　　　　　LP: EMI 1C 147 01633-01634M

Serse, Largo

March 1950　　　　　　　　　　　　78: Columbia DX 1681
　　　　　　　　　　　　　　　　　45: Columbia SED 5507/SCD 2086

HAMILTON HARTY (1879-1941)

The Fair Day (Irish Symphony)

October 1962　　　　　　　　　　　45: HMV 7P 394
　　　　　　　　　　　　　　　　　LP: HMV CLP 1645/CSD 1495
　　　　　　　　　　　　　　　　　LP: World Records T 927/ST 927

FRANZ JOSEF HAYDN (1732-1809)

Trumpet Concerto

June 1946　　Mortimer　　　　　　78: Columbia DX 1535-1536
　　　　　　　　　　　　　　　　　78: Columbia (Italy) GQX 11212-11213
　　　　　　　　　　　　　　　　　45: Columbia SCD 2005

The Spirit's Song (Hark what I tell thee)

May 1946　　Ripley　　　　　　　　78: HMV C 3500
　　　　　　　　　　　　　　　　　LP: EMI HLM 7145

GUSTAV HOLST (1874-1934)

St Paul's Suite

September
1953

LP: Columbia 33S 1100
LP: EMI XLP 30049

Jupiter (The Planets)

May 1961

LP: Columbia 33SX 1436/SCX 3446
LP: EMI XLP 30049

Somerset Rhapsody

September
1953

LP: Columbia 33S 1100

Marching Song (Songs Without Words)

September
1953

LP: Columbia 33S 1100
LP: EMI XLP 30049
XLP 30049 names orchestra as LSO

ENGELBERT HUMPERDINCK (1854-1921)

Hänsel und Gretel, Dream Pantomime

November
1951

78: Columbia DX 1811
45: Columbia SCD 2013

MIKHAIL IPPOLITOV-IVANOV (1859-1935)

Procession of the Sardar (Caucasian Sketches)

July 1951

78: Columbia DX 1792
45: Columbia SED 5522
LP: Columbia 33SX 1032

196 Weldon

FRANZ LISZT (1811-1886)

Hungarian Rhapsody No 2

March 1953   78: Columbia DX 1886
                              45: Columbia SCD 2131
                              LP: Columbia 33SX 1032

PIETRO MASCAGNI (1863-1945)

Cavalleria rusticana, Intermezzo

November   78: Columbia DX 1807
1951   78: Columbia (Germany) DWX 5073
                              45: Columbia SED 5518
                              LP: Columbia 33SX 1032

JULES MASSENET (1842-1912)

Thais, Méditation for violin and orchestra

July 1951   Parikian   78: Columbia DX 1792

NIKOLAI MEDTNER (1879-1951)

Piano Concerto No 1

September-   Medtner   78: HMV DB 6900-6904/DB 9379-9383
November   LP: Melodiya M10 41169-41170/
1947   D 16313-16314

FELIX MENDELSSOHN-BARTHOLDY (1809-1847)

Hebrides Overture

March 1956	LP: Columbia 33SX 1054
	LP: EMI MFP 2037

A Midsummer Night's Dream, Scherzo

August 1945	HMV unpublished
May 1961– April 1963	LP: Columbia 33SX 1570/SCX 3499

War March of the Priests (Athalie)

November 1951	78: Columbia DX 1818
	78: Columbia (Germany) DWX 5078
	LP: Columbia (USA) RL 3042

GIACOMO MEYERBEER (1791-1864)

Coronation March (Le prophète)

July 1951	78: Columbia DX 1801
	78: Columbia (Germany) DWX 5075

LEOPOLD MOZART (1719-1787)

Toy Symphony (Cassation in G)

July 1951	78: Columbia DX 1784
	45: Columbia SED 5509/SCD 2098

WOLFGANG AMADEUS MOZART (1756-1791)

Le nozze di Figaro, Overture

May 1961   LP: Columbia 33SX 1436/SCX 3446

OTTO NICOLAI (1810-1849)

Die lustigen Weiber von Windsor, Overture

March 1956   LP: Columbia 33SX 1054
                                      LP: EMI MFP 2037

JACQUES OFFENBACH (1819-1880)

Orfée aux enfers, Overture

November   78: Columbia DX 1823
1951   78: Columbia (Germany) DWX 5077
                                      78: Columbia (Italy) GQX 16654
                                      45: Columbia SED 5552

AMILCARE PONCHIELLI (1834-1886)

Dance of the Hours (La Gioconda)

March 1956   LP: Columbia 33SX 1054
                                      LP: EMI MFP 2037

SERGEI PROKOFIEV (1891-1953)

L'amour des 3 oranges, March

May 1961   LP: Columbia 33SX 1436/SCX 3446

CAMILLE SAINT-SAENS (1835-1921)

Danse macabre

March 1956   LP: Columbia 33SX 1054
                            LP: EMI MFP 2037

Samson et Dalila, Bacchanale

March 1956   LP: Columbia 33SX 1054
                            LP: EMI MFP 2037

JEAN SIBELIUS (1865-1957)

Finlandia

March 1956   LP: Columbia 33SX 1054
                            LP: EMI MFP 2037

BEDRICH SMETANA (1824-1884)

The Bartered Bride, Dance of the Comedians

May 1961   LP: Columbia 33SX 1436/SCX 3446

The Bartered Bride, Polka

April 1963   LP: Columbia 33SX 1570/SCX 3499

FRANZ VON SUPPE (1819-1895)

Light Cavalry, Overture

March 1953   78: Columbia DX 1873
                            45: Columbia SCD 2108
                            LP: Columbia 33SX 1032

PIOTR TCHAIKOVSKY (1840-1893)

Piano Concerto No 1

August 1945	Moiseiwitsch	78: HMV C 3466-3470/C 7623-7627

1812 Overture

May 1963	Royal Marines' Band	LP: Columbia 33SX 1570/SCX 3499 LP: EMI XLP 30123/SXLP 30123

The Sleeping Beauty, Complete ballet

March- May 1956	LP: Columbia 33SX 1095-1096 LP: EMI CFPD 4458 CD: EMI CDCFPD 4458 Excerpts LP: EMI XLP 30012/SXLP 30012

The Sleeping Beauty, Waltz

November 1951	78: Columbia DX 1807 78: Columbia (Germany) DWX 5073 45: Columbia SED 5518 LP: Columbia 33SX 1032

Waltz (Serenade for strings)

April 1963	LP: Columbia 33SX 1570/SCX 3499 LP: EMI XLP 30123/SXLP 30123

RALPH VAUGHAN WILLIAMS (1872-1958)

Fantasia on Greensleeves

May 1961   LP: Columbia 33SX 1436/SCX 3446
            LP: EMI XLP 30123/SXLP 30123/CFP 4510

March (Folk Songs from Somerset)

October   LP: HMV CLP 1645/CSD 1495
1962   LP: World Records T 927/ST 927

GIUSEPPE VERDI (1813-1901)

La traviata, Act 1 Prelude

April 1963   LP: Columbia 33SX 1570/SCX 3499

RICHARD WAGNER (1813-1883)

Tannhäuser, Entry of the Guests

May 1963   LP: Columbia 33SX 1570/SCX 3499

WILLIAM WALTON (1902-1983)

Orb and Sceptre, March

October   45: HMV 7P 388
1962   LP: HMV CLP 1645/CSD 1495
            LP: World Records T 927/ST 927

Weldon

TRADITIONAL AND MISCELLANEOUS

Devonshire Cream and Cider; In summertime on Bredon; David of the White Rock; Blow the Wind Southerly; An Eriskay Love Lilt

| October 1962 | Harvey | LP: HMV CLP 1645/CSD 1495 |
| | | LP: World Records T 927/ST 927 |

God Save the Queen, arranged by Walton (1953)

April 1956   Columbia unpublished

God Save the Queen, arranged by Walton (1955)

April 1956   Columbia unpublished

Robert Irving
1913-1995

PHILHARMONIA
ORCHESTRA

COLUMBIA

1951-52 CATALOGUE

~ the finest name on record

ADOLPHE ADAM (1803-1856)

Giselle, standard abridged version

May 1961
LP: HMV CLP 1589/CSD 1465
LP: EMI CFP 41 45051
<u>Excerpts</u>
LP: EMI XLP 30087/SXLP 30087

MALCOLM ARNOLD (Born 1921)

English Dances

June 1953
LP: HMV CLP 1172

Homage to the Queen, Suite

June 1953
LP: HMV CLP 1011

Scottish Dances

June 1957
LP: HMV CLP 1172
LP: World Records T 725/ST 725
LP: EMI CFP 40308

BELA BARTOK (1881-1945)

The Miraculous Mandarin, Ballet suite

June 1961
LP: Capitol P 8576/SP 8576

Irving

BENJAMIN BRITTEN (1913-1976)

Matinées musicales, Ballet suite

June 1957   LP: HMV CLP 1172
                                       LP: World Records T 725/ST 725
                                       LP: EMI CFP 40308

Soirées musicales, Ballet suite

June 1957   LP: HMV CLP 1172
                                       LP: World Records T 725/ST 725
                                       LP: EMI CFP 40308

FRÉDÉRIC CHOPIN (1810-1849)

Les Sylphides, Ballet suite arranged by Douglas

April 1959   LP: HMV CLP 1296/CSD 1271
                                       LP: World Records T 964/ST 964
                                       Excerpts
                                       LP: EMI XLP 30087/SXLP 30087

LEO DELIBES (1836-1891)

Coppélia, Ballet suite

June 1960   Menuhin   LP: HMV ALP 1869/ASD 439
                                       LP: EMI CFP 124

Sylvia, standard abridged version

April 1954   LP: HMV CLP 1058
                                       Excerpts
                                       45: HMV 7EP 7046/7EP 7053

Sylvia, Ballet suite

June 1960   Menuhin   LP: HMV ALP 1869/ASD 439
                                       LP: EMI CFP 124

ERNO DOHNANYI (1877-1960)

Suite for orchestra

June 1954   LP: HMV CLP 1043

CHARLES GOUNOD (1818-1893)

Faust, Ballet music

September   78: HMV C 7932-7933
1952

GIOACHINO ROSSINI (1792-1868)

La boutique fantasque, arranged by Respighi

September   LP: HMV DLP 1032
1952

ROBERT SCHUMANN (1810-1856)

Carnaval, Ballet suite arranged by Jacob

October   LP: HMV CLP 1013
1952   One of the few EMI recordings carried out
                             in Royal Festival Hall

April 1959   LP: HMV CLP 1296/CSD 1271
                             LP: World Records T 964/ST 964
                             Excerpts
                             LP: EMI XLP 30087/SXLP 30087

Irving

DIMITRI SHOSTAKOVICH (1906-1975)

The Age of Gold, Ballet suite

June 1961   LP: Capitol P 8576/SP 8576

PIOTR TCHAIKOVSKY (1840-1893)

Hamlet, Fantasy Overture

June 1954   LP: HMV CLP 1043
                                    LP: EMI XLP 30036

Swan Lake, Excerpts

May 1953   LP: HMV CLP 1018

INDEX OF COMPOSERS AND WORKS

This listing summarises the recorded repertoire of the Philharmonia Orchestra under the conductors featured in these discographies. Numbers after each work refer to the pages on which an entry occurs. The term "excerpts" covers overtures, arias or any other extract from a larger musical work.

Adam Giselle
205

Albinoni Oboe Concerto No 6
45

Oboe Concerto No 3 - excerpt
45

Arnold English Dances
205

Scottish Dances
205

Scottish Dances - excerpt
187

Homage to the Queen
205

Auber La muette de Portici - excerpt
11

J.C.Bach Sinfonia in B flat
45

Bach Ach Gott vom Himmel sieh darein
139

Air (Suite No 3)
187

Cantata No 51
45

Cantata No 51 - excerpt
187

Cantata No 82
45

Concerto in C for 2 pianos
11

Concerto for 2 violins
46, 153

Oboe Concerto, arranged by Tovey
46

Oboe Concerto in A
46

Piano Concerto in D minor
46

Saint Matthew Passion - excerpt
46

Schafe können sicher weiden
187

Suite No 2
46

Violin Concerto in A minor
47

Violin Concerto in E
47, 153

Balakirev Islamey
131

Overture on Russian themes
131

Russia
131

Tamar
131

Barber Adagio for strings
79, 139

Souvenirs, suite
139

Bartok Miraculous Mandarin, suite
205

Beethoven Symphony No 5
115

Symphony No 7
11

Piano Concerto No 1
12

Piano Concerto No 2
12, 115

Piano Concerto No 3
12, 47, 115

Piano Concerto No 4
13, 115

Piano Concerto No 5
13, 47

Violin Concerto
11

Violin Romances Nos 1 and 2
47, 79

Coriolan Overture
79, 99

Egmont Overture
14

Fidelio - excerpts
14, 47

German Dances Nos 11 and 12
47

Die Geschöpfe des Prometheus Overture
99

Leonore No 3 Overture
79, 99, 115

Die Ruinen von Athen - excerpt
139

Bellini Capuleti ed i Montecchi - excerpt
169

Norma - excerpt
48

La sonnambula - excerpts
14, 169

Berg Violin Concerto
79

Berlioz Beatrice & Benedict Overture
80

Benvenuto Cellini Overture
80

Carnaval romain Overture
80, 116

Le corsair Overture
80

La damnation de Faust - excerpts
48, 140, 187

Les francs juges Overture
81

Les troyens - excerpt
140

Bizet L'arlésienne - excerpts
81

Carmen - excerpts
14, 48

Les pêcheurs de perles - excerpt
15

Bloch Violin Concerto
81

Boccherini Minuetto
99, 188

Boito Mefistofele - excerpts
48, 99, 116

Borodin Symphony No 1
15

Symphony No 2
81, 100

Symphony No 3
100

Prince Igor - excerpts
100, 116, 117, 131, 132, 169

Nocturne
169

Brahms Piano Concerto No 2
117, 170

Violin Concerto
82, 117, 170

Double Concerto
15, 82

Haydn Variations
82

Hungarian Dances - excerpts
82, 83, 188

Tragic Overture
15, 82

Bruch Violin Concerto No 1
49, 170

Das Feuerkreuz - excerpt
49

Britten Matinées & soirées musicales
206

Bruckner Symphony No 4
132

Overture in G minor
132

Scherzo (Symphony No 0)
132

Catalani Loreley - excerpt
16

La wally - excerpts
16, 49

Chabrier Joyeuse marche
140

Charpentier Louise - excerpts
118, 170

Chausson Poème
118, 170

Chopin Piano Concerto No 1
16, 83

Piano Concerto No 2
83

Autumn Leaves, ballet
140

Les sylphides, suite
206

Cilea Adriana Lecouvreur - excerpts
50

L'arlesiana - excerpt
17

Clarke Trumpet Voluntary
188

Coates London Suite - excerpt
188

Oxford Street - excerpt
188

Coleridge-Taylor Petite suite de concert
188

Davies Solemn Melody
189

Debussy La mer
17

Nocturnes
17, 18

Prélude à l'après-midi d'un faune
18

Délibes Coppélia, suite
206

Lakmé - excerpt
18

Pas de Naila
100

Sylvia
206

Sylvia - excerpts
189, 206

Delius Koanga - excerpt
189

Dohnanyi Cello Concerto
50

Suite for orchestra
207

Variations on a Nursery Song
170

Donizetti L'elisir d'amore - excerpts
18, 50

La favorita - excerpt
18

Don Pasquale - excerpt
171

Dukas L'apprenti sorcier
19

Dvorak Symphony No 9
19, 100

Cello Concerto
51

Carnival Overture
189

Cunning Peasant Overture
51

Rusalka - excerpts
51

Scherzo capriccioso
51

Slavonic Dances
101

Elgar Cockaigne Overture
190

Enigma Variations
190

Pomp & Circumstance Marches 1 and 4
190

Sea Pictures
190

Falla El amor brujo - excerpt
191

El sombrero de 3 picos, suite
19

Fauré Elégie for cello and orchestra
52

Flotow Martha - excerpt
19

Franck Symphony in D minor
20

Variations symphoniques
52, 191

Giordano Andrea Chenier - excerpts
20, 52, 118

Glazunov Violin Concerto
133

Raymonda - excerpts
101, 133

Les ruses d'amour - excerpts
101

The Seasons - excerpts
101, 141

Stenka Razin
171

Valse de concert No 1
171

Les vendredis
101

Glière The Red Poppy - excerpt
102

Glinka Jota aragonesa
84, 102

Kamarinskaya
84

A Life for the Tsar - excerpts
141

Ruslan and Ludmila - excerpts
84, 102, 191

Valse Fantaisie
102

Gluck Alceste - excerpt
171

Iphigénie en Aulide - excerpt
171

Orfeo ed Euridice - excerpt
53

Goossens Oboe Concerto
53

Gounod Faust - excerpts
53, 141, 172, 207

Mors et vita - excerpt
102

La reine de Saba - excerpt
53

Roméo et Juliette - excerpts
20, 53

Grainger Londonderry Air
191

Mock Morris
191

Granados Goyescas - excerpts
54, 172, 192

Grieg Piano Concerto
21, 153

Elegaic Melodies
54, 173, 192

Holberg Suite
173, 192

Lyric Suite
55

Norwegian Dances
54, 173

Norwegian Melodies
192

Peer Gynt - excerpts
54, 173

Sigurd Jorsalfar suite
192

Symphonic Dances
54, 55, 118, 173

Varen
55

Handel Organ Concerto in B flat
55

Berenice - excerpt
193

Giulio Cesare - excerpt
193

Joshua - excerpt
193

Messiah - excerpts
174, 193

Orlando - excerpt
193

Samson - excerpt
194

Serse - excerpt
194

Harty Irish Symphony - excerpt
194

Haydn Symphony No 100
153

Symphony No 104
119

Trumpet Concerto
194

Violin Concerto in C
55

Serenade
103

Spirit's Song
194

Hérold Zampa Overture
84, 103

Heuberger Der Opernball - excerpt
154

Holst Jupiter (The Planets)
195

Marching Song
195

Saint Paul's Suite
195

Somerset Rhapsody
195

Honegger Concertino for piano and orchestra
174

Humperdinck Hänsel und Gretel - excerpt
195

Ippolitov-Ivanov Caucasian Sketches
84, 103

Caucasian Sketches - excerpt
195

Kabalevsky The Comedians suite
141

Khachaturian Gayaneh - excerpts
103

Maskerade - excerpts
141

Korngold Die tote Stadt - excerpt
55

Lalo Symphonie espagnole
56

Lehar Der Graf von Luxemburg - excerpt
154

Giuditta - excerpt
154

Das Land des Lächelns
155

Die lustige Witwe
133, 155

Der Zarewitsch - excerpt
155

Liadov Baba Yaga
104

Russian Folksong
104, 119

Lincke Lysistrata - excerpt
142

Liszt Piano Concerto No 1
156, 174

Piano Concerto No 2
56

Hungarian Fantasia
56, 156

Hungarian Rhapsody No 2
56, 196

Mazeppa
174

Les Préludes
21, 174

Totentanz
174

Litolff Scherzo (Concerto symphonique)
57

Lortzing Der Waffenschmied - excerpt
156

Der Wildschütz - excerpt
156

Zar und Zimmermann - excerpt
157

Mahler Symphony No 4
85

Symphony No 5 - excerpt
85

Das Lied von der Erde
85

Marcello Oboe Concerto in D minor
57

Mascagni L'amico Fritz - excerpt
119

Cavalleria rusticana - excerpts
57, 196

Guglielmo Ratcliff - excerpt
22

Le maschere Overture
22

Massenet Manon - excerpts
22. 58, 175

Thais - excerpts
58, 196

Werther - excerpt
22

Medtner Piano Concerto No 1
196

Piano Concerto No 2
120

Piano Concerto No 3
120

Mendelssohn Violin Concerto
23, 85, 142, 175

Capriccio brillant
104

Athalie - excerpt
197

Hebrides Overture
58, 86, 104, 197

Heimkehr aus der Fremde Overture
86

A Midsummer Night's Dream Incidental music
85

A Midsummer Night's Dream - excerpt
197

Ruy Blas Overture
86, 104

Songs without Words - excerpts
104

Meyerbeer Le prophète - excerpts
142, 197

Robert le diable - excerpt
175

Milhaud Piano Concerto No 1
175

Cello Concerto
59

Millöcker Die Dubarry - excerpts
157

Leopold Mozart Toy Symphony
197

Mozart Piano Concerto No 9
59

Piano Concerto No 12
105

Piano Concerto No 15
158

Piano Concerto No 20
59

Piano Concerto No 24
59, 143

Piano Concerto No 27
143

Concerto for 2 pianos
23

Horn Concerto No 2
59

Flute Concerto No 1
143

Flute Concerto No 2
143

Andante for flute and orchestra
143

Violin Concerto No 1
60

Violin Concerto No 2
60

Violin Concerto No 3
60, 158

Violin Concerto No 4
60

Violin Concerto No 5
60

Ascanio in Alba - excerpt
23

Ch'io mi scordi di te?
158

Così fan tutte - excerpts
23, 60

Don Giovanni - excerpts
24, 60

Die Entführung aus dem Serail - excerpt
24

Exsultate jubilate
61

Exsultate jubilate - excerpt
23

La finta semplice - excerpt
24

Mass in C minor - excerpt
24

Misera dove son?
24, 61

Nehmt meinen Dank
24

Le nozze di Figaro - excerpts
25, 61, 120, 198

Il rè pastore - excerpt
25

Zaide - excerpt
25

Die Zauberflöte - excerpt
25

Mussorgsky Boris Godunov - excerpts
62, 105, 120, 121

The Capture of Kars - excerpt
62

Intermezzo in B minor
62

Khovantschina - excerpts
25, 62, 86, 105, 121, 122

Night on Bare Mountain
62, 86, 105, 133

Scherzo in B flat
62

Song of the Flea
122

Sorochinsky Fair - excerpts
62, 105

Nicolai Die lustigen Weiber von Windsor Overture
86, 175, 198

Offenbach Orphée aux enfers Overture
158, 198

Paganini Violin Concerto No 1
134

Violin Concerto No 2
176

Pick-Mangiagalli Notturno romantico
26

Pizzetti La pisanella
26

Ponchielli La Gioconda - excerpt
26, 198

Prokofiev Symphony No 1
106, 144

Symphony No 5
86

Symphony No 7
106

Piano Concerto No 1
63

Piano Concerto No 3
63

Violin Concerto No 2
26

Cello Concerto
63

Lieutenant Kije - excerpt
176

The Love of 3 Oranges suite
106, 144, 198

Peter and the Wolf
144

Romeo and Juliet - excerpts
144

Puccini La Bohème - excerpts
27, 63, 122

La fanciulla del West - excerpt
63

Madama Butterfly - excerpts
27, 64

Manon Lescaut - excerpt
64

Tosca - excerpt
64

Turandot - excerpts
27, 65

Rachmaninov Piano Concerto No 1
106

Piano Concerto No 2
28, 106, 158

Piano Concerto No 3
28, 65, 87

Paganini Rhapsody
65

Ravel Bolero
87

Daphnis et Chloé, 2nd suite
28

Pavane pour une infante défunte
87

Tzigane
159

Respighi Impressioni brasiliane
28

Fontane di Roma
28

Rezniceck Donna Diana Overture
176

Rimsky-Korsakov Piano Concerto
177

Baba Yagar
177

Capriccio espagnol
29

Le coq d'or - excerpts
29, 122, 145

Dubinushka
145

Ivan the Terrible Overture
107

May Night Overture
177

The Prophet
123

Russian Easter Festival Overture
123, 134

Sadko - excerpt
123

Scheherazade
87, 122, 134

Skaska
177

Snow Maiden - excerpts
107, 145, 177

Tsar Sultan - excerpts
87, 107, 123, 145

Rossini La boutique fantasque
31, 207

Il barbiere di Siviglia
30

Il barbiere di Siviglia Overture
31

La Cenerentola Overture
31

La gazza ladra Overture
31

Guglielmo Tell Overture
31

L'italiana in Algeri Overture
32

La scala di seta Overture
32

Semiramide Overture
32

Il signor bruschino Overture
32

Rubinstein Melody in F
145

Saint-Saens Cello Concerto No 1
66

Violin Concerto No 3
177

Le carnaval des animaux
146

Le carnaval des animaux - excerpt
146

Danse macabre
199

Etienne Marcel - excerpt
66

Havanaise
33

Samson et Dalila - excerpts
66, 123, 199

Domenico Scarlatti Oboe Concerto
66

Schnabel Rhapsody for orchestra
90

Schubert Symphony No 5
33

Symphony No 8
90

Rosamunde Incidental music
90

Marche militaire
146

Schumann Piano Concerto
33, 159

Carnival Ballet suite
207

Scriabin Piano Concerto
123

Shostakovich Symphony No 1
146

Symphony No 10
146

The Age of Gold suite
146, 208

Sibelius Symphony No 1
91

Symphony No 2
91

Symphony No 3
91

Violin Concerto
66

En Saga
91

Finlandia
107, 199

Valse triste
91

Sieczinsky Wien du Stadt meiner Träume
159

Smetana The Bartered Bride - excerpts
67, 92, 199

Dalibor - excerpt
67

From Bohemia's Woods and Fields
159

The Moldau
159

Sousa Stars and Stripes Forever
147

Johann Strauss I Radetzky March
147

Johann Strauss II Casanova - excerpt
160

Die Fledermaus
160

Frühlingsstimmen
67

Eine Nacht in Venedig
160

Eine Nacht in Venedig - excerpt
161

Wiener Blut
161

Der Zigeunerbaron
161

Der Zigeunerbaron - excerpt
161

Josef Strauss Sphärenklänge
92

Richard Strauss Arabella - excerpts
135

Burleske
178

Capriccio - excerpt
162

Don Juan
34

Horn Concerto No 1
34

Horn Concerto No 2
34

Oboe Concerto
34

Tod und Verklärung
34

4 letzte Lieder
162

Stravinsky Petrushka
147

L'oiseau de feu suite
33

2 Suites for orchestra
147

Suppé Beautiful Galatea Overture
92

Boccaccio - excerpt
162

Light Cavalry Overture
92, 199

Morning Noon and Night in Vienna Overture
92

Pique Dame Overture
92

Poet and Peasant Overture
107

Taneyev Suite de concert
108

Tartini Concertino
67

Tchaikovsky Symphony No 4
108, 124

Symphony No 5
93

Symphony No 6
93, 108

Manfred Symphony
93

Piano Concerto No 1
35, 124, 200

Violin Concerto
35, 68, 178

Suite No 3 - excerpt
108

Suite No 4
179

Serenade for strings
93, 124

Serenade for strings - excerpt
200

1812 Overture
108, 200

Andante cantabile
94, 178

Capriccio italien
35, 94

Casse noisette suite
109, 148

Evgeny Onegin - excerpts
35, 68, 124, 178

Hamlet
135, 178, 208

Iolanta - excerpt
178

The Maid of Orleans - excerpt
68

Marche slave
148

Mazeppa - excerpt
110

Pique Dame - excerpt
68

Romeo and Juliet
35, 178

Russian Dance
148

Sérénade mélancolique
162

The Sleeping Beauty
200

The Sleeping Beauty - excerpts
109, 148, 200

The Slippers suite
179

The Storm Overture
135, 179

Swan Lake - excerpts
148, 179, 208

Voyevoda - excerpt
110

Turina Cantares
69

Rapsodia sinfonica
69

Saeta
69

Vaughan Williams Oboe Concerto
69

Folksongs from Somerset - excerpt
201

Greensleeves
201

Verdi Aida - excerpts
36, 70, 125, 149

Ave Maria
179

Un ballo in maschera - excerpts
70, 125

Don Carlo - excerpts
125, 179

Ernani - excerpt
179

La forza del destino - excerpts
36, 70, 125, 180

Luisa Miller Overture
36

Nabucco - excerpts
37, 180

Otello - excerpts
37, 71, 125

Requiem - excerpt
70

Rigoletto - excerpts
37, 70

Simone Boccanegra - excerpt
181

La traviata - excerpts
38, 71, 181, 201

Il trovatore - excerpt
38

I vespri siciliani Overture
38, 181

Vieuxtemps Violin Concerto No 4
71

Violin Concerto No 5
181

Vivaldi Oboe Concerto in D minor
71

Wagner Der fliegende Holländer - excerpts
72, 94, 110, 163

Lohengrin - excerpts
72, 94, 95, 126, 163, 181

Meistersinger von Nürnberg Overture
126

Parsifal - excerpts
126, 163

Siegfried Idyll
39, 95

Tannhäuser - excerpts
39, 72, 73, 95, 126, 127, 163, 181, 201

Träume (Wesendonk-Lieder)
95

Tristan und Isolde - excerpts
95, 127

Die Walküre - excerpts
73, 163

Walton Orb and Sceptre march
201

Weber Konzertstück
39

Beherrscher der Geister Overture
73

Der Freischütz - excerpts
73, 74

Oberon - excerpts
74, 110

Weinberger Polka and Fugue
95

Wolf Italian Serenade
74

Wolf-Ferrari Gioielli della madonna intermezzo
40, 182

I quattro rusteghi intermezzo
40

Il segreto di Susanna Overture
40, 182

Zandonai Giulietta e Romeo - excerpt
40

Zeller Der Obersteiger - excerpt
164

Der Vogelhändler - excerpt
164

Discographies

The Furtwängler Sound, 5th edition
Composer and chronological discographies,
300 pages
Price £22 (£28 outside UK)

Teachers and pupils
Schwarzkopf / Ivogün / Cebotari /
Seinemeyer / Welitsch / Streich / Berger
7 separate discographies, 400 pages
Price £22 (£28 outside UK)

The post-war German tradition
Kempe / Keilberth / Sawallisch /Kubelik /
Cluytens
5 separate discographies, 300 pages
Price £22 (£28 outside UK)

**Mid-century conductors
and More Viennese singers**
Böhm / De Sabata / Knappertsbusch / Serafin /
Krauss / Dermota / Rysanek / Wächter /
Reining / Kunz
10 separate discographies, 420 pages
Price £18 (£22 outside UK)

Leopold Stokowski
Discography and concert register, 300 pages
Price £22 (£28 outside UK)

Tenors in a lyric tradition
Fritz Wunderlich / Walther Ludwig /
Peter Anders
3 separate discographies, 350 pages
Price £22 (£28 outside UK)

A notable quartet
Janowitz / Ludwig / Gedda / Fischer-Dieskau
4 separate discographies, 600 pages
Price £20 (£25 outside UK)

Musical knights
Wood / Beecham / Boult / Barbirolli /Goodall /
Sargent
6 separate discographies, 400 pages
Price £20 (£25 outside UK)

Prices include postage
order from: John Hunt, Flat 6,
37 Chester Way, London SE11 4UR

Music and Books published by Travis & Emery Music Bookshop:
Anon.: Hymnarium Sarisburiense, cum Rubricis et Notis Musicis.
Agricola, Johann Friedrich from Tosi: Anleitung zur Singkunst.
Bach, C.P.E.: edited W. Emery: Nekrolog or Obituary Notice of J.S. Bach.
Bateson, Naomi Judith: Alcock of Salisbury
Bathe, William: A Briefe Introduction to the Skill of Song
Bax, Arnold: Symphony #5, Arranged for Piano Four Hands by Walter Emery
Burney, Charles: The Present State of Music in France and Italy
Burney, Charles: The Present State of Music in Germany, The Netherlands ...
Burney, Charles: An Account of the Musical Performances ... Handel
Burney, Karl: Nachricht von Georg Friedrich Handel's Lebensumstanden.
Cobbett, W.W.: Cobbett's Cyclopedic Survey of Chamber Music. (2 vols.)
Corrette, Michel: Le Maitre de Clavecin
Crimp, Bryan: Dear Mr. Rosenthal ... Dear Mr. Gaisberg ...
Crimp, Bryan: Solo: The Biography of Solomon
d'Indy, Vincent: Beethoven: Biographie Critique
d'Indy, Vincent: Beethoven: A Critical Biography
d'Indy, Vincent: César Franck (in French)
Frescobaldi, Girolamo: D'Arie Musicali per Cantarsi. Primo & Secondo Libro.
Geminiani, Francesco: The Art of Playing the Violin.
Handel; Purcell; Boyce; Geene et al: Calliope or English Harmony: Volume First.
Häuser: Musikalisches Lexikon. 2 vols in one.
Hawkins, John: A General History of the Science and Practice of Music (5 vols.)
Herbert-Caesari, Edgar: The Science and Sensations of Vocal Tone
Herbert-Caesari, Edgar: Vocal Truth
Hopkins and Rimboult: The Organ. Its History and Construction.
Hunt, John: Adam to Webern: the recordings of von Karajan
Isaacs, Lewis: Hänsel and Gretel. A Guide to Humperdinck's Opera.
Isaacs, Lewis: Königskinder (Royal Children) A Guide to Humperdinck's Opera.
Kastner: Manuel Général de Musique Militaire
Lacassagne, M. l'Abbé Joseph : Traité Général des élémens du Chant.
Lascelles (née Catley), Anne: The Life of Miss Anne Catley.
Mainwaring, John: Memoirs of the Life of the Late George Frederic Handel
Malcolm, Alexander: A Treaty of Music: Speculative, Practical and Historical
Marx, Adolph Bernhard: Die Kunst des Gesanges, Theoretisch-Practisch
May, Florence: The Life of Brahms
May, Florence: The Girlhood Of Clara Schumann: Clara Wieck And Her Time.
Mellers, Wilfrid: Angels of the Night: Popular Female Singers of Our Time
Mellers, Wilfrid: Bach and the Dance of God
Mellers, Wilfrid: Beethoven and the Voice of God
Mellers, Wilfrid: Caliban Reborn - Renewal in Twentieth Century Music

Music and Books published by Travis & Emery Music Bookshop:
Mellers, Wilfrid: François Couperin and the French Classical Tradition
Mellers, Wilfrid: Harmonious Meeting
Mellers, Wilfrid: Le Jardin Retrouvé, The Music of Frederic Mompou
Mellers, Wilfrid: Music and Society, England and the European Tradition
Mellers, Wilfrid: Music in a New Found Land: ... ... American Music
Mellers, Wilfrid: Romanticism and the Twentieth Century (from 1800)
Mellers, Wilfrid: The Masks of Orpheus: ...... the Story of European Music.
Mellers, Wilfrid: The Sonata Principle (from c. 1750)
Mellers, Wilfrid: Vaughan Williams and the Vision of Albion
Panchianio, Cattuffio: Rutzvanscad Il Giovine
Pearce, Charles: Sims Reeves, Fifty Years of Music in England.
Playford, John: An Introduction to the Skill of Musick.
Purcell, Henry et al: Harmonia Sacra ... The First Book, (1726)
Purcell, Henry et al: Harmonia Sacra ... Book II (1726)
Quantz, Johann: Versuch einer Anweisung die Flöte traversiere zu spielen.
Rameau, Jean-Philippe: Code de Musique Pratique, ou Methodes.
Rastall, Richard: The Notation of Western Music.
Rimbault, Edward: The Pianoforte, Its Origins, Progress, and Construction.
Rousseau, Jean Jacques: Dictionnaire de Musique
Rubinstein, Anton : Guide to the proper use of the Pianoforte Pedals.
Sainsbury, John S.: Dictionary of Musicians. Vol. 1. (1825). 2 vols.
Serré de Rieux, Jean de : Les dons des Enfans de Latone
Simpson, Christopher: A Compendium of Practical Musick in Five Parts
Spohr, Louis: Autobiography
Spohr, Louis: Grand Violin School
Tans'ur, William: A New Musical Grammar; or The Harmonical Spectator
Terry, Charles Sanford: J.S. Bach's Original Hymn-Tunes for Congregational Use.
Terry, Charles Sanford: Four-Part Chorals of J.S. Bach. (German & English)
Terry, Charles Sanford: Joh. Seb. Bach, Cantata Texts, Sacred and Secular.
Terry, Charles Sanford: The Origins of the Family of Bach Musicians.
Tosi, Pierfrancesco: Opinioni de' Cantori Antichi, e Moderni
Van der Straeten, Edmund: History of the Violoncello, The Viol da Gamba ...
Van der Straeten, Edmund: History of the Violin, Its Ancestors... (2 vols.)
Waltern: Musikalisches Lexicon
Walther, J. G.: Musicalisches Lexikon ober Musicalische Bibliothec

Travis & Emery Music Bookshop
17 Cecil Court, London, WC2N 4EZ, United Kingdom.
Tel. (+44) 20 7240 2129

© Travis & Emery 2009

Discographies by Travis & Emery:
Discographies by John Hunt.

1987: 978-1-906857-14-1: From Adam to Webern: the Recordings of von Karajan.
1991: 978-0-951026-83-0: 3 Italian Conductors and 7 Viennese Sopranos: 10 Discographies: Arturo Toscanini, Guido Cantelli, Carlo Maria Giulini, Elisabeth Schwarzkopf, Irmgard Seefried, Elisabeth Gruemmer, Sena Jurinac, Hilde Gueden, Lisa Della Casa, Rita Streich.
1992: 978-0-951026-85-4: Mid-Century Conductors and More Viennese Singers: 10 Discographies: Karl Boehm, Victor De Sabata, Hans Knappertsbusch, Tullio Serafin, Clemens Krauss, Anton Dermota, Leonie Rysanek, Eberhard Waechter, Maria Reining, Erich Kunz.
1993: 978-0-951026-87-8: More 20th Century Conductors: 7 Discographies: Eugen Jochum, Ferenc Fricsay, Carl Schuricht, Felix Weingartner, Josef Krips, Otto Klemperer, Erich Kleiber.
1994: 978-0-951026-88-5: Giants of the Keyboard: 6 Discographies: Wilhelm Kempff, Walter Gieseking, Edwin Fischer, Clara Haskil, Wilhelm Backhaus, Artur Schnabel.
1994: 978-0-951026-89-2: Six Wagnerian Sopranos: 6 Discographies: Frieda Leider, Kirsten Flagstad, Astrid Varnay, Martha Moedl, Birgit Nilsson, Gwyneth Jones.
1995: 978-0-952582-70-0: Musical Knights: 6 Discographies: Henry Wood, Thomas Beecham, Adrian Boult, John Barbirolli, Reginald Goodall, Malcolm Sargent.
1995: 978-0-952582-71-7: A Notable Quartet: 4 Discographies: Gundula Janowitz, Christa Ludwig, Nicolai Gedda, Dietrich Fischer-Dieskau.
1996: 978-0-952582-75-5: Leopold Stokowski (1882-1977): Discography and Concert Register
1996: 978-0-952582-76-2: Makers of the Philharmonia: 11 Discographies: Alceo Galliera, Walter Susskind, Paul Kletzki, Nicolai Malko, Issay Dobrowen, Lovro Von Matacic, Efrem Kurtz, Otto Ackermann, Anatole Fistoulari, George Weldon, Robert Irving.
1996: 978-0-952582-72-4: The Post-War German Tradition: 5 Discographies: Rudolf Kempe, Joseph Keilberth, Wolfgang Sawallisch, Rafael Kubelik, Andre Cluytens.
1996: 978-0-952582-73-1: Teachers and Pupils: 7 Discographies: Elisabeth Schwarzkopf, Maria Ivoguen, Maria Cebotari, Meta Seinemeyer, Ljuba Welitsch, Rita Streich, Erna Berger.
1996: 978-0-952582-75-5: Leopold Stokowski: Discography and Concert Listing.
1996: 978-0-952582-76-2: Makers of the Philharmonia: 11 Discographies Alceo Galliera, Walter Susskind, Paul Kletzki, Nicolai Malko, Issay Dobrowen, Lovro Von Matacic, Efrem Kurtz, Otto Ackermann, Anatole Fistoulari, George Weldon, Robert Irving.
1996: 978-0-952582-77-9: Tenors in a Lyric Tradition: 3 Discographies: Peter Anders, Walther Ludwig, Fritz Wunderlich.
1997: 978-0-952582-78-6: The Lyric Baritone: 5 Discographies: Hans Reinmar, Gerhard Huesch, Josef Metternich, Hermann Uhde, Eberhard Waechter.
1997: 978-0-952582-79-3: Hungarians in Exile: 3 Discographies: Fritz Reiner, Antal Dorati, George Szell.
1997: 978-1-901395-00-6: The Art of the Diva: 3 Discographies: Claudia Muzio, Maria Callas, Magda Olivero.
1997: 978-1-901395-01-3: Metropolitan Sopranos: 4 Discographies: Rosa Ponselle, Eleanor Steber, Zinka Milanov, Leontyne Price.
1997: 978-1-901395-02-0: Back From The Shadows: 4 Discographies: Willem Mengelberg, Dimitri Mitropoulos, Hermann Abendroth, Eduard Van Beinum.
1997: 978-1-901395-03-7: More Musical Knights: 4 Discographies: Hamilton Harty, Charles Mackerras, Simon Rattle, John Pritchard.
1998: 978-1-901395-95-2: More Giants of the Keyboard: 5 Discographies: Claudio Arrau, Gyorgy Cziffra, Vladimir Horowitz, Dinu Lipatti, Artur Rubinstein.

1998: 978-1-901395-94-5: Conductors On The Yellow Label: 8 Discographies: Fritz Lehmann, Ferdinand Leitner, Ferenc Fricsay, Eugen Jochum, Leopold Ludwig, Artur Rother, Franz Konwitschny, Igor Markevitch.
1998: 978-1-901395-96-9: Mezzo and Contraltos: 5 Discographies: Janet Baker, Margarete Klose, Kathleen Ferrier, Giulietta Simionato, Elisabeth Hoengen.
1999: 978-1-901395-97-6: The Furtwaengler Sound Sixth Edition: Discography and Concert Listing.
1999: 978-1-901395-98-3: The Great Dictators: 3 Discographies: Evgeny Mravinsky, Artur Rodzinski, Sergiu Celibidache.
1999: 978-1-901395-99-0: Sviatoslav Richter: Pianist of the Century: Discography.
2000: 978-1-901395-04-4: Philharmonic Autocrat 1: Discography of: Herbert Von Karajan [Third Edition].
2000: 978-1-901395-05-1: Wiener Philharmoniker 1 - Vienna Philharmonic and Vienna State Opera Orchestras: Discography Part 1 1905-1954.
2000: 978-1-901395-06-8: Wiener Philharmoniker 2 - Vienna Philharmonic and Vienna State Opera Orchestras: Discography Part 2 1954-1989.
2001: 978-1-901395-07-5: Gramophone Stalwarts: 3 Separate Discographies: Bruno Walter, Erich Leinsdorf, Georg Solti.
2001: 978-1-901395-08-2: Singers of the Third Reich: 5 Discographies: Helge Roswaenge, Tiana Lemnitz, Franz Voelker, Maria Mueller, Max Lorenz.
2001: 978-1-901395-09-9: Philharmonic Autocrat 2: Concert Register of Herbert Von Karajan Second Edition.
2002: 978-1-901395-10-5: Sächsische Staatskapelle Dresden: Complete Discography.
2002: 978-1-901395-11-2: Carlo Maria Giulini: Discography and Concert Register.
2002: 978-1-901395-12-9: Pianists For The Connoisseur: 6 Discographies: Arturo Benedetti Michelangeli, Alfred Cortot, Alexis Weissenberg, Clifford Curzon, Solomon, Elly Ney.
2003: 978-1-901395-14-3: Singers on the Yellow Label: 7 Discographies: Maria Stader, Elfriede Troetschel, Annelies Kupper, Wolfgang Windgassen, Ernst Haefliger, Josef Greindl, Kim Borg.
2003: 978-1-901395-15-0: A Gallic Trio: 3 Discographies: Charles Muench, Paul Paray, Pierre Monteux.
2004: 978-1-901395-16-7: Antal Dorati 1906-1988: Discography and Concert Register.
2004: 978-1-901395-17-4: Columbia 33CX Label Discography.
2004: 978-1-901395-18-1: Great Violinists: 3 Discographies: David Oistrakh, Wolfgang Schneiderhan, Arthur Grumiaux.
2006: 978-1-901395-19-8: Leopold Stokowski: Second Edition of the Discography.
2006: 978-1-901395-20-4: Wagner Im Festspielhaus: Discography of the Bayreuth Festival.
2006: 978-1-901395-21-1: Her Master's Voice: Concert Register and Discography of Dame Elisabeth Schwarzkopf [Third Edition].
2007: 978-1-901395-22-8: Hans Knappertsbusch: Kna: Concert Register and Discography of Hans Knappertsbusch, 1888-1965. Second Edition.
2008: 978-1-901395-23-5: Philips Minigroove: Second Extended Version of the European Discography.
2009: 978-1-901395--24-2: American Classics: The Discographies of Leonard Bernstein and Eugene Ormandy.

Discography by Stephen J. Pettitt, edited by John Hunt:
1987: 978-1-906857-16-5: Philharmonia Orchestra: Complete Discography 1945-1987

Available from: Travis & Emery at 17 Cecil Court, London, UK. (+44) 20 7 240 2129. email on sales@travis-and-emery.com .

© Travis & Emery 2009

www.ingramcontent.com/pod-product-compliance
Lightning Source LLC
Chambersburg PA
CBHW070942230426
43666CB00011B/2524